MW00948298

SINGLE
AND
WHOLE

A God-Focused Life

RUTH WILCOX

WESTBOW
PRESS®
A DIVISION OF THOMAS NELSON
& ZONDERVAN

Copyright © 2016, 2017 Ruth Wilcox.

All rights reserved. No part of this book may be used or reproduced by any means, graphic, electronic, or mechanical, including photocopying, recording, taping or by any information storage retrieval system without the written permission of the author except in the case of brief quotations embodied in critical articles and reviews.

This book is a work of non-fiction. Unless otherwise noted, the author and the publisher make no explicit guarantees as to the accuracy of the information contained in this book and in some cases, names of people and places have been altered to protect their privacy.

Scripture quotations marked NASB are taken from the New American Standard Bible®, Copyright© 1960, 1962, 1963, 1968, 1971, 1972, 1973, 1975, 1977, 1995 byThe Lockman Foundation. Used by permission.

Scripture quotations marked NIV are taken from the Holy Bible, New International Version®. NIV®. Copyright © 1973, 1978, 1984 by International Bible Society. Used by permission of Zondervan. All rights reserved.

Scripture quotations marked NKJV are taken from the New King James Version. Copyright © 1982 by Thomas Nelson, Inc. Used by permission. All rights reserved.

Scripture quotations from The Holy Bible, English Standard Version® (ESV®). Copyright ©2001 by Crossway Bibles, a division of Good News Publishers. Used by permission. All rights reserved.

Scripture quotations marked NLT are taken from the Holy Bible, New Living Translation, copyright © 1996, 2004, 2007. Used by permission of Tyndale House Publishers, Inc. Carol Stream, Illinois 60188. All rights reserved. Website

WestBow Press books may be ordered through booksellers or by contacting:

WestBow Press
A Division of Thomas Nelson & Zondervan
1663 Liberty Drive
Bloomington, IN 47403
www.westbowpress.com
1 (866) 928-1240

Because of the dynamic nature of the Internet, any web addresses or links contained in this book may have changed since publication and may no longer be valid. The views expressed in this work are solely those of the author and do not necessarily reflect the views of the publisher, and the publisher hereby disclaims any responsibility for them.

Any people depicted in stock imagery provided by Thinkstock are models, and such images are being used for illustrative purposes only.
Certain stock imagery © Thinkstock.

ISBN: 978-1-5127-8303-2 (sc)
ISBN: 978-1-5127-8304-9 (hc)
ISBN: 978-1-5127-8302-5 (e)

Library of Congress Control Number: 2017905526

Print information available on the last page.

WestBow Press rev. date: 4/18/2017

Dedicated to

My Sisters in Christ

CONTENTS

JOURNEY OF PURPOSE

How do I write this? I am not a writer by any means, and my grammar is normally atrocious. But friend, I have been feeling that God desires to speak on a particular subject to a particular group of people—single women, including me. He wants to speak to our hearts about the purpose of our lives and how we daily choose to live. Also, He wants us to recognize our worth and find true fulfillment.

Many women, young and old, are looking to other people for their fulfillment. Why not? That is what the world teaches us to do, and not just the world, but sometimes our families also. In conversation, it's usually not blatant, but rather a subtle undertone. "When are you getting married?" "Anyone special in your life?" We're asked these questions by well-meaning people who genuinely love us and have our well-being at heart. Yet such questions condition us to expect another person to enter our lives—an elusive person who we allow to partly determine our worth, whether we realize this or not. As Christians, we should not let others determine our worth or purpose in life.

You might be asking, "Are you married, to be able to speak in authority about this?" No, I'm not. However I'm not speaking about marriage per se, but more about *not* being married, a topic on which I consider myself an expert. Too many women, including Christian women, base their worth and future on an elusive future husband who, honestly, not all women will ever have. Many women are married, of course, and to those of you who are, I hope you also gain something from this book. Most of what I am about to share comes from the perspective of an unmarried life, but I will touch on many aspects of living as a Christian woman, married or not. I would like to present the things that God has taught me and those things that I am daily surrendering to Him as I learn to live as His beloved and dedicate my life to Him, the lover of my life, heart, and spirit.

Allow me to offer a disclaimer. It is highly possible that as you're reading this, you will become frustrated, confused, or perhaps even angry. The premise and purpose of this book is not to soothe, but to awaken. Some of you might experience—as I did while writing this book—a tearing down of several assumptions that have been perpetuated by your own hopes, families, and even the church. I would ask you to hold on tight, be patient, and allow the Holy Spirit to direct you.

This book was not written for the faint of heart, but for women who have a deep desire to become one with the Creator of the universe. Such women are willing to stand up boldly, as Esther did, and surrender everything to Jesus for the time that has been given to them. We are called to give our lives for Christ, to live in Him and with His Spirit, to be His vessels, to be powerful women of faith, like the Shunammite woman who laid all her hopes and dreams before her God and would not let Him go. (See 2 Kings 4:8–37.) I pray that if you feel a desire to read this book, it is because the Holy Spirit is drawing you into a deeper understanding in this area of your life.

I ask that you not take this next sentence as a promise or prophetic declaration regarding your life, but instead accept it as a bridge that must be crossed in the early part of our journey. You and I might never be married. There is an extremely good chance that such will be the case for *at least* one person reading this book, although only God knows whom that might be.

Still there? Now that I've roundhouse kicked you in the face, allow me to apply a balm to your wound. This might not seem overly encouraging at first, but it is true that in Christ, you are *already* whole. We tend to assume that as long as we're single, we remain in a holding pattern, waiting to meet Mr. Right. However, you need to understand and embrace, as best as you can, the fact that God has a reason for your unmarried state. You may indeed be called to marry one day, but being single makes you no less of a person. Right now you are called to live *fully* with Jesus just as you are—single and whole.

So let's start this journey of tearing down these assumptions that the world, people around us, and even we ourselves have established. Let us ask the Holy Spirit to breathe life into us, building new understanding and hope.

1

Every Girl's Desire

Arise, shine; for your light has come,
And the glory of the Lord has risen upon you.
For behold, darkness will cover the earth
And deep darkness the peoples;
But the Lord will rise upon you.
Nations will come to your light,
And kings to the brightness of your rising.
—Isaiah 60:1–3

As a Child

All women were once little girls. Think back to that time in your life. What was important to you? What did you play with, and whose attention did you crave? We might not have all been the typical little girl most people envision when they talk about girls four to ten years old. By *typical*, I mean the little girl in a princess dress, twirling her skirts and trying on her mother's makeup and jewelry. Typical little girls dress up to get attention from the important people in their lives and hear them say, "You are adored. We love to look at you."

As one of these typical little girls, I loved dresses and jewels. At the age of five, it was not uncommon for me to dance in front of strangers. At seven, I could often be seen twirling the skirt of my dress, no matter who was around (or how visible my underwear was). I was innocent and carefree, as a child should be. I expressed my desire to be adored by

1

dressing in beautiful clothes and dancing or singing for any audience. My heart was looking for affirmation of who I was, not as a prideful thing, but because of an inherent need for affirmation and approval. God builds this desire into our very foundation.

Our hearts cry out for approval and affirmation. Often we seek these from multiple sources aside from God, but that's not necessarily bad. In God's infinite kindness, He gives us people and things as symbols and trail markers to point us to Himself as the fulfillment of our hearts' desires. We have certain relationships here on earth (parents, spouses, friends, and so on) to point us to the *ultimate* relationship. In these earthly relationships, our longing to be welcomed in and accepted can be signposts to point us to the One from whom genuine approval and affirmation comes.

Too often, we look for these from almost anyone except God, from whom we really need them. We seek people's love and approval, but we don't work on developing our understanding of Jesus's love for us—and thus a better understanding of His *approval* of us. In fact, this approval and affirmation we need *must* come from Him. In Matthew 25:21, we see that our destiny is determined by six critical words of approval: "Well done, good and faithful servant."

As young children, our pursuit of ultimate approval begins in the midst of the people around us.

Not All Seem the Same

I had honestly never considered that other girls wouldn't like all that girlie stuff I loved as a child. Over time, however, through conversations I've had with good friends and observations of people around me, I have come to understand that some girls were different. One of my best friends told me that while she was growing up, she dressed in boyish clothes and shunned anything with the "look of a girl." She always felt out of place, as though she wasn't normal because she didn't like feminine things. She was concerned that her lack of interest in girlie activities made her less of a true girl. Another one of my best friends says that she always felt masculine and too tall, and her awkwardness caused her to shun makeup and "froufrou" things.

The world makes us think that we should act like everyone else and appreciate the same things as everyone else. (Who is everyone else?) If we don't, then we are to be treated differently from the rest of the crowd—strange, outcast, and rejected. Uncool. Unfortunately, sometimes this ends up being true. Many people have bought into this way of thinking, including little girls who have doubts about who they are and fears about being perceived as odd.

We perpetually fear being excluded from the "inner ring," a concept that C. S. Lewis mentions in *The Weight of Glory:* "I believe that in all men's lives at certain periods, and in many men's lives at all periods between infancy and extreme old age, one of the most dominant elements is the desire to be inside the local Ring and the terror of being left outside."[1]

My friend's less-than-girlie ways always made her feel like an odd duck. She wondered if something was actually wrong with her and whether she needed to change to fit the standard female mold. She wondered then—and continues to wonder today—if her desires were the same as those of other women, or whether she would always be abnormal. Were the things meant for other women not meant for her? She felt abandoned on the outside of her "local Ring."

God-Given Desires

I believe some innate desires are really God-given desires and others are not. Whether we consider ourselves princess-dress girls or hoodie-and-Converse girls, these desires are part of what makes each of us unique.

---

[1] C. S. Lewis, *The Weight of Glory,* p. 146.

would pay attention to which desires are holy and pure and which
are not.

Our personalities and desires start to be expressed from a young
age. When they do, we begin to realize some are good and pure (ones
from God), and others show our fallen nature. We can look at a child
and see only a sweet and innocent child, but when she starts to talk, she
can be rude or self-absorbed.

I remember my sister-in-law telling me that after my two-year-old
nephew, whom I love very much, was disciplined, he looked her in the
eyes and said, "Mom, I'm thinking of a way to hurt you." He was two!
He did not learn this from anyone; his parents are not violent and don't
speak in threatening ways. He also had been sheltered by his parents
from most outside influences, so he was just beginning to understand
the world. My nephew is very smart and loving, but even at the age of
two he struggled with a sinful nature.

I agree when the scriptures say that we are all corrupt from the
moment we are created in our mothers' wombs. Psalm 51:5 says, "Surely
I was sinful at birth, sinful from the time my mother conceived me"
(NIV). We are all in need of Jesus's full redemptive work from the
moment we are conceived, and we're born with sin clinging to us.
Christ's forgiveness is needed by everyone, no matter our age, and we
do not need more redemption as we age.

As we grow older, we learn ways to act on the sin in our hearts.
Everyone's sin is somewhat different, just as we all have different
struggles and passions. Some people think that because they were born
with a certain affinity or inclination, that automatically grants them
blessing in doing whatever they please in that area. However, being
born with a desire to be greedy or violent doesn't mean that acting
on those desires is righteous. It is the same for any desire that does
not line up with scripture, innate or not, including things such as
homosexuality, sex outside marriage, pride, lying, and so many others.
We are held accountable for what we do with these desires by God's
Word and His commandments. God does not give us commandments

to follow because we are perfect. Instead, He has made His commands of righteousness known to us so that we will see where we are going wrong, so that we can see where we need His help to change.

What does a young girl typically talk about? What is important to her? She wants to be adored and appreciated for who she is, know someone who loves her, and have people or things to take care of and nurture. Granted, these three desires are more subdued for some girls than for others. But I still believe they are present for every girl to some extent, and as we grow, we look for ways to fulfill these desires.

I was one of those girls who wanted to dress up in pretty things. My children were stuffed animals, and with my dolls I acted out scenes of being loved and pursued. I exhibited all three desires—to be adored, to have someone to take care of, and to be loved. But as I grew older, the desire to be adored turned into, "I want people to think I'm pretty."

At the young age of nine, I started to think I wasn't pretty enough to be adored. I had started to buy into the non-Christian world's idea that nobody would notice me or show me affection unless I was beautiful. As years went by, I felt even less beautiful. I gained weight, thus administering another kick to my feeling of self-worth, which was already lying broken on the floor. Through a vicious cycle, my opinion of myself was gradually poisoned. When the world whispered to me that thin and sexy are beautiful, and that if I couldn't hit the mark, the world didn't want to know me ... I listened.

I hid away and isolated myself from the world, trying to protect the inner me from being rejected again. As a college student, I stayed in my room, afraid of being judged on my appearance and scared of being thought unintelligent if I opened my mouth to speak. My self-worth was wrapped up in what the world thought I should be. I was also outside of my "local Ring." I listened to the world's words of rejection even though I was told that God loves me the way I am.

Friend, God does love us just the way we are, but this such a basic view of how God thinks of us. There is much more depth to Him than this, and yet this statement is also true in its simplicity. We will discuss in another chapter who we really are and how God views us.

Our Family's Role

Our parents play a crucial part in how we grow to see ourselves. They are our original role models for how we should behave, how a woman should be treated, what she should look for in her life, and even how God views us. Our parents don't always accurately reflect Him to us, but that is the inevitable result of growing up with any authority other than God Himself. How we come to think of God is often shaped by our view of our parents. Our mothers are examples, as women of God, of who we could become and how we can love others.

Our fathers, on the other hand, play a large role in how we see our value, because they have the power to give us the approval we desire. They can help us become stronger women, or they can make us feel as small as a child, no matter our age. Our father's powerful influence on us, whether negative or positive, will affect how we see ourselves, and therefore also how we let others treat us.

Women who never had a father around may find it more difficult to understand the difference a father makes, or they might be able to see the obvious hole left in his absence. One way or another, our fathers have a great effect on who we become. No parent is perfect, so let's cut them some slack where we can. But if our parents do their jobs well, they help us start to understand our true worth.

The World's Influence On Our Desires

As a Christian, I struggled with how to be a good Christian girl and yet be sexy so that the world would adore me. There are a few things wrong with this thinking. First, the idea of being sexy for anyone other than our husbands is unholy and degrading. We were never meant to be devalued to just what pleasure our bodies can give or on how pleasing we look. Women are vessels of God, "fearfully and wonderfully made" (Psalm 139:14). Second, Jesus says that we "are not of the world" (John 17:14). We are in the world, just as He was in the world, but we are not of the world, just as He was not of the world. Even though we live in the world, we are not meant to look, sound, or think like non-Christians, and because of this, people will hate us. As Jesus says in Mark 13:13, "You will be hated by all because of my name."

This may sound harsh to our easy Western mind-set, for we have become lazy in many areas. Most important, we have become lazy about living in relationship with Christ and therefore living for Christ. But if we open our eyes to what is going on in other parts of the world, we will see that the world does hate us. History has shown how the world treats those who love God. Examples include the Roman Colosseum; the underground church in China; Christians in Iran; and present-day ISIS torturing, raping, and beheading Christians. And if we pay attention to what is happening in America, we will notice people becoming bolder in their persecution of Christians.

If we try to meld the world's values and standards with those of God, we end up with a life that is "neither hot nor cold" (Revelation 3:16–18). Think of a hot drink, perhaps tea or coffee, steaming and delightful. (I prefer a drink to almost burn my mouth, because I find it more satisfying.) Then add a few ice cubes, just enough to bring the drink to room temperature—bland, boring, and unsatisfying. This is what we become when we mix our ice cold world with the hot, empowering life of God's Spirit.

One of the overwhelmingly intense messages with which this world tries to indoctrinate us is the message that if we want to experience a full life, we will need a spouse to help us achieve it. This is one of the mind-sets that I bought into for years without even realizing it.

As a child, if I had been asked which I wanted more, a husband or children, my answer would have been a husband—and this desire has not diminished as I've grown older. I always thought that I would surely be married by the age of twenty. I have struggled with my lack of a spouse for years, often thinking that if I only had a husband, I would feel loved and satisfied with life. Over the years, I've seen most of my friends get married and have families of their own—constantly reminding me of my own singleness.

Since most of my friends now have children, my life no longer easily fits with theirs, unless I'm willing to babysit or do kid-friendly things. Girlfriends of mine, don't presume that I don't want to be with you and love on you and your kids. It's just that my life and yours are in very different stages, and I cannot relate to everything that you care about. I have not had to think through all the issues of wifehood, much less motherhood.

Now my twenties are gone, and nothing has changed in this respect except my understanding. I am now beginning to see who I truly am, for whom I am supposed to live, and how my life should look. This understanding has come through reading God's Word and through the illuminating breath of the Holy Spirit. And this understanding isn't just for me—God wants all of His girls to understand His heart and live life to the fullest in Him.

God is not holding us back from a fulfilling life. We choose to be held back from that life. We need to open our eyes and our hearts to Jesus.

Bringing Us Back Into Focus

Maybe you have never thought about this before, but everything you desire and expect from life comes from some foundational source: God, the world, or some combination that results from the fall in Eden. Every fire is caused by a spark, and every expectation has a root. We must be careful to examine what we build our expectations on. If we build on the world, we are bound to be disappointed and always looking for something more. With the combination, we are still on very dangerous ground, because when we start to mix God's promises with the world's promises, we end up blaming God for breaking promises He never really made. Or we become disappointed because we expect promises to be answered quickly, but then that doesn't always happen. Then we can easily end up like Abraham and Sarah, taking things into our own hands to find a way to help God keep His promise. (See Genesis 16.) God can keep His promises without our help. He will use us, but we really need to be completely open to His leading, including His timing. Sometimes we must be willing to just stand patiently and let the Lord show His greatness in our lives. Things might take longer than we had hoped or anticipated, but that does not mean it will not happen. God's "word is not void" (Isaiah 55:11).

God-given desires for us will be fulfilled as long as we live our lives fully submitted to Him, although maybe not fulfilled in the way that we expect. He does not call us to have selfish expectations for our lives, but to set our expectations on Him—that He will be holy, good, just, and faithful. All else in our lives should take a place of lesser importance, really meaning *no* importance except as He gives it. Nothing in this world has any lasting value apart from Jesus. Only if we live through Him will He groom and cultivate our desires and hopes. He will bless not only us, but also the world through us.

As we consider our expectations, what have we allowed to be at the root of who we are? Upon what do we base our entire world? Upon what are we basing our beliefs? I hope we have discovered our only foundation to be Jesus, the only true source of life. If we build on anything less than Jesus, the Word of Life, our lives will end up like the house in the New Testament that toppled and fell "and the ruin of that house was great" (Luke 6:49).

My best friend, whom I mentioned earlier, recently shared that God is teaching her who He is, and through this she is learning who she is in Him. When we begin to see ourselves as He sees us, we learn who we truly are in Christ. This light brings clarity to how we should live and what really has eternal importance. As my friend begins to see herself through God's eyes, she better understands that He made her the way she is—including her boyish likes and such—for a purpose. But she is also learning to bring to His feet the parts of her that do not line up with the holiness of God and let Him burn away the wretched parts. This is something we must all do, if we desire to live and have our being in Him. We cannot skip this process.

2

HOW THE CHURCH HAS FAILED

> But we all, with unveiled face, beholding as in a mirror
> the glory of the Lord, are being transformed into the same image
> From glory to glory, just as from the Lord, the Spirit.
> —2 Corinthians 3:18

Who Is the Church?

If we have given our lives to Jesus and asked for His redemption from our sins, making Him Lord in our lives, then we have become God's children and sisters to Christ. (See Romans 8:17.) In this huge transition from hell to heaven, we have also been given a new family of brothers and sisters, as well as some new father and mother figures. These people are what Christians refers to as the *church*.

The scriptures also say we are "the body of Christ," with all parts united to make up the whole. (See 1 Corinthians 12:27.) And because all together—not just our churches, but all churches—we make up the body of Christ, all people who are in Christ, no matter where they are in the world, are part of the church. So *the church* could mean our local group of believers or the whole body of Christ, which includes everyone who has made Jesus their Lord. When Saul persecuted the church, he was persecuting the body of Christ. (See Acts 8:3.)

Many of us refer to the building in which we meet as a church, and that isn't an inaccurate use of the word. But for our purposes in this book, we will use *church* to mean a group of people who gather together to worship God—just as Christ meant it in saying that He would build His church. (See Matthew 16:18.)

Why Does It Matter What They Say?

Typically, the people we look to for community are the people who tend to influence us, whether we really notice their influence or not. When I spend time with specific people, the way they act rubs off on me. Sometimes I find myself talking and laughing like a person with whom I'm spending my time, or I use the same exclamations they do. When I catch myself, I'm surprised at how moldable I am to the people around me.

To some extent, we are all like this. Even if we try to just be ourselves, often we end up caring about the same things as the people around us. Over time, we tend to see life through their eyes and accept their viewpoints to one degree or another.

The people whom we choose to be around also make a difference in how we see ourselves. Those to whom we look for guidance do just that: they guide the way we think, which in turn influences how we live our lives. Eventually, they influence what we expect from life and how we expect a Christian woman to look.

Our lives are like picture puzzles made up of differently shaped and colored pieces that represent our beliefs and experiences. We create works of art with our lives. Each is a unique masterpiece, although many of our puzzle pieces are influenced by those around us. We take ideas— puzzle pieces—from various people. But sometimes we splash different colors on them to make them our own, although we don't change their shapes. By taking bits and pieces from different sources in our lives, we end up creating a puzzle of our own beliefs, expectations, and hopes. Whether we notice it or not our end result is still greatly influenced by those we surround ourselves with, so it's important to have people in our lives who encourage us and help guide us in the right direction.

Having a mentor can be invaluable, but few of us have anyone to take on that specific role.

When Christ ascended into heaven after His resurrection, He promised to send us a counselor and teacher, the Holy Spirit. (See John 14:26.) Whether or not we have a human mentor, the Holy Spirit is here and available, through the grace and love of Jesus, to show us how to live. Unfortunately most of us have not learned how to hear the Holy Spirit in our lives. We crowd Him out with distractions, worries, selfishness, cultural influences, and so on, which silences His voice of influence within us. That's what I did for years, but by the grace of God, I will never do so again.

A Caution

I want to take what to some might seem like a detour. But we are only as strong as our foundations, and we are only as powerful and free in our lives as the concepts and beliefs we have chosen. So here it goes.

We have a tendency to accept whatever comes from the pulpit as gospel truth. I'm not suggesting that we shouldn't believe anything said from the pulpit, because our pastors and others who speak from the pulpit have been chosen for a reason. They deserve our respect and honor. We are *always* to respect people in authority over us.

However, we should be mindful and weigh out everything we hear and see, even from the pulpit, according to the Bible. Jude says, "For certain persons have crept in unnoticed, those who were long beforehand marked out for this condemnation, ungodly persons who turn the grace of our God into licentiousness and deny our only Master and Lord, Jesus Christ" (Jude 1:4).

A few verses earlier in Jude, the writer says he is addressing "the called, beloved in God the Father, and kept for Jesus Christ" (Jude 1:1). So this letter was written to a Christian community of believers, not to nonbelievers. Now notice that Jude 1:4 includes the words *unnoticed, ungodly*, and *licentiousness*. We might think that if a false prophet or teacher got into the church, we would know it, but this scripture clearly says the people who crept in were completely unnoticed. They simply blended in with the holy congregation of God. They couldn't even be recognized as different from those who claimed to believe in God.

Not only did they blend in, but they were ungodly, and they were in a position to influence this church group with licentiousness. *Licentious* means "unrestrained by law or general morality; immoral."[2] These ungodly people took liberties with the grace of God. They did whatever they wanted and expected God's grace to cover their sin, thus denying the Lordship of Christ through disobedience.

Sometimes we tell ourselves that we're not really choosing sin over God when we commit just a small sin. But honestly, no sin is small. Jesus died on the cross because of every sin, regardless of how small it might seem. And if Jesus isn't in authority over us as Lord of our lives, then we can't have salvation. Christ cannot be duped. He knows our hearts, and salvation comes only to those who are repentant and proclaim Jesus as Lord. (See Romans 10:9.) When we declare Him as Lord, with our words and obedience, He will give us grace to turn away from the sinfulness that is now dead in our lives. Praise God!

With this grace, we are also to test the spirit of everything we hear and see. (See 1 John 4:1.) People in authority can easily misdirect us if we are not careful to test the information they give against the scripture. If what we have been told does not hold up to the Bible, it is not something we should use to guide our lives. As 2 Timothy 3:16–17 says, "All Scripture is inspired by God and profitable for teaching, for reproof, for correction, for training in righteousness; so that the man of God may be adequate, equipped for every good work."

All scripture is given by God to guide us into all truth. Scripture is the only standard against which everything should be measured—past, present, and future. With this understanding in place, let's continue.

---

[2] Dictionary.com.

Have We Been Given a Lost Battle?

Have you ever noticed that most books for Christian women are focused on married women? They're usually written from the perspective of a married Christian woman, so I often have to remind myself to read them in a general light. I ask myself how the author's point might be applied to my relationships with people other than a spouse. Instead of respecting my nonexistent husband, for example, I try to respect people who have authority over various aspects of my life, such as work or church. This can be exhausting, like always being told how to fix my motorcycle when actually I have a moped. It doesn't always translate well.

I have talked with other single Christian women, and they all say the same thing. We feel forgotten and lost. The writers give us just one page out of a 160-page book, and even then, the focus is on how to prepare for when it's time for us to get married. Or the church tells us, "Why don't you come to the singles group? You might find your future spouse there." Or maybe, "We have this book on preparing your heart for your future spouse."

Even our families tend to offer helpful advice about how to find a boyfriend or "get out there more." They want to see us married and having kids, which I'm sure most of us wouldn't mind. But their expectation that we *should* be married often leaves us feeling incomplete, as though something is wrong with us and what we are doing as single women.

Honestly, we need to get this straight. If God meant for us to be married right now, He would have provided the right person for us. He is more than capable and wants the best for us, though often our idea of best doesn't line up with His.

I believe the church responds this way because they don't really know what to tell us or how to help, so they just say to patiently wait for our spouse. We've all heard something like this: "God is just preparing you and your future husband to find each other." The problem is that this belief could be setting us up for future failure. The church wants to give us hope of being married one day, but "hope deferred makes the heart sick" (Proverbs 13:12). Maybe they're encouraging us to hope for something for which we should *not* be looking, because it's the wrong focus for us right now.

Because I adopted this focus from those I respected, my heart has been sick for many years, creating much bitterness. No one ever told me I might not get married or that I needed to make Jesus my all in all in this area. No one said I should look to God for fulfillment in all things, or at least I never imagined that God could be enough to completely fill my desire for a relationship. I wasn't counseled to seek Him fully in this area, but only to *use* God to prepare me for my actual husband.

I am not saying we shouldn't get married or hope for marriage in our futures. But the church has held marriage up as the main goal for which women should strive, and this focus on a spouse—instead of Jesus—sets us up for constant failure. We have no control over whether or when we will get married; that is in God's hands. And we should not desire a husband so much that it becomes the focus of our lives and hearts. The only thing we should hope for is to love completely and give our lives in full surrender to Christ. He should be our waking passion and the purpose that guides our lives, even in this deeply personal area.

I don't mean to condemn the church or stir up anger, but to help women understand why we are so confused on this subject—and how we can and should go forward with our lives.

Where We Have Gotten Lost?

Almost from the beginning of time, women have been dealt a hard hand. In the garden of Eden, we were cursed with the desire for a husband. (See Genesis 3:16.) Actually I believe that curse was meant to draw us closer to God. Our longing for a husband is meant to point us to our deeper need for Christ. Everything God does has a purpose and is done to draw us to Him. According to the Bible, husbands represent the groom (Jesus) and wives represent the bride of Christ, in what is meant only as a small, shadow version of the relationship between Christ and His church. (See Ephesians 5:22–33.)

We have allowed ourselves to focus on the earthly shadow things that seem so real to us, but we must remember to do as directed in scripture: "Therefore if you have been raised up with Christ, keep seeking the things above, where Christ is, seated at the right hand of God. Set your mind on the things above, not on the things that are on earth. For you have died and your life is hidden with Christ in God" (Colossians 3:1–3).

Some might say that God is meant for the spiritual side of things, and the earth is meant for the physical. Not so. God is meant for all. He created all and is in all. I am not talking about New Age thinking, in which God is one with the trees and leaves, but if we are aware of it, everything can point us to Him. God is sovereign over everything. Nothing has its being without His life-giving power, nor does anything happen that He does not allow. If we can't comprehend our need for God enough to seek our satisfaction in Him alone, we will never find it. No one else can completely satisfy us. We might be placated for a time, but that will eventually wear off and we'll end up wanting more. A husband can give us only part of what we really desire. Placing all our expectations on our husbands will eventually produce frustration in our marriages. Husbands are not—and can never be—the Lovers of our souls. Truly understanding this requires the awakening of the Holy Spirit.

In my own life, it took the Holy Spirit's power and my commitment. Being halfhearted never works, so I gave all to God. It took months of walking out this choice before I started to really understand its power. Even now, I still have to commit to it every day. In return, however, God has committed Himself completely to me. This relationship with God is a beautiful, everlasting covenant.

What Do We Really Need?

Can you not guess my answer? (I wanted to put a smiley face here.) What we really need is a burning desire for God, which comes only when the Holy Spirit draws us and we respond by daily choosing to seek Him for who He is. This is the only place a true, deep relationship with God can be created. We must come to Him desiring His presence, not what He can give us. If we approach the throne of God with an underlying desire for a husband, rather than for God, He will know. He knows our hearts, desires, and thoughts. (See Psalm 139:1–4.) He sees every part of who we are. He desires such a deep intimacy with us, one we can experience only with Him. He wants us to seek Him alone, to desire to look upon only His face. God wants us to know what brings Him joy and makes Him weep. We see this in its purest form when David says in Psalm 27:8, "You have said to me 'Seek my face.' Your face, O Lord, do I seek."

Our desire for God will allow Him to burn away everything in our lives that does not bow to His authority. If we want to be able to truly say, "I am my beloved's and my beloved is mine" (Song of Solomon 6:3), then we must desire Him above all else, including the comfort another person might give us. God wants to be that comfort and wholeness for us.

It seems almost impossible to think that we can find everything that we desire in God alone. But that's like saying that God is not God—that He is not all powerful, all present, and all knowing. It doesn't make sense to think that we need God's creation to give us something that God, the creator, can't provide. Don't get me wrong—I am *not* referring to a sexual relationship with God. Definitely not. I am saying, however, that He can satisfy our needs and desires more than we could ever fathom, even in this area.

God knows exactly what we need, and He can fill our needs in ways we never expected—or help quiet them when necessary. God will always be around to provide our needs, because He will never die. "He will be with you. He will not fail you or forsake you" (Deuteronomy 31:8). And anyway, how dare we give things or people in our lives more power than God! Maybe I sound a little harsh, but this is *God* we are talking about. Our excuses will not stand before Him.

Don't get me wrong—I know this is much easier said than done. I have struggled for years, and I still have my moments. So I am preaching to myself just as much, if not more, than to anyone else. The world is tangible and constantly before my eyes, which makes it easy to fall back on, but God is much closer than I often recognize. As Jesus tells us, "With God all things are possible" (Matthew 19:26). Notice that Jesus says *all* things are possible, not just *some* things. But we must relinquish our own strength and become completely dependent on God.

Unfortunately there don't seem to be many single Christian women living lives of faith in this area of their relationships. I am not saying that there aren't many wonderful, single Christian women in this world who are serving our Lord. However, there seem to be disproportionately more broken women who are hurting and lost, and who have turned to the world and other people to satisfy their deep desire and need for wholeness. Some godly examples exist here and there, but not many understand the importance of looking to God, first and foremost, to fill the void in their hearts. If only we could see that when we focus on Him wholeheartedly, our wounds will be healed and our questions will be answered.

What Are We Choosing?

Eve's fall in the garden of Eden brought several curses upon all women: "I will greatly multiply your pain in childbirth, in pain you will bring forth children; yet your desire will be for your husband, and he will rule over you" (Genesis 3:16). I'm not going to discuss the part about husbands ruling over their wives, which is a separate issue, nor will I get into the topic of painful childbirth. But I do want to discuss the desire of women for a husband.

We can see from the Bible that our desire for companionship is natural and universal. Before Eve was created, Adam searched for a companion. He noticed that all other creatures had partners just like themselves, but he could not find another of his kind. This desire for fellowship with one another is a basic human characteristic given to us by God. In fact, before the world was created, the Trinity existed in unity and fellowship. God gave us this part of Himself when He made us in His image—not just His physical image, but an image encompassing God's spirit, soul, and body.

But when humankind sinned in the garden of Eden, God told Eve that she would now desire her husband. So in addition to our normal desire for companionship, we now have a strong desire for a husband. As a result, women tend to be most comfortable when we have a man around, which helps us feel safe and secure. Think about it. How many of our girlfriends talk about their dislike of being alone? When a girl breaks up with her boyfriend, she almost immediately goes out with another guy, right? Or maybe we know women who stay with guys just because they don't want to be alone—guys who aren't kind or respectful, and who demand ungodly things from women. We all have a deep yearning to be with someone and an innate dislike of being alone. But this is God's way of drawing us to Himself, if only we would see this and choose Him.

We need to be careful not to use other things to satisfy our desire for a husband, including church programs, events, or gatherings. I don't mean that we shouldn't be involved in the church or programs the church provides, because a church community is very important for all believers. However, we need to look to the scriptures and draw on our relationship with Christ as the true fulfillment of our need for companionship. Only through Jesus will we gain freedom in this area, and the longer we avoid this understanding, the longer we will feel empty. This isn't always an easy process, but Christ can make it easier for us, if we're willing to die to what we have come to expect and open our hearts to what He wants to give.

I have struggled for years to come to the point of surrender in this area of my life. I've always wanted someone with whom to share my life, because I thought that would fill my loneliness. I was unwilling to give this desire to God and let Him work through it to create a deep desire for Jesus and therefore satisfaction in Him. To be honest, I didn't really think it was possible to be satisfied in Him alone. I always expected that if I surrendered my desire for a husband to Him, I would still feel alone and have to die daily to this desire. This didn't sound like fun, but a few years ago I knew it was time to give Him all areas of my life, including this one. I didn't want to just *say* I was doing so, and then maybe someday ask for it back, but instead to completely hand it over to Him and expect only Him in return.

So I did, and—truth be told—I still didn't feel satisfaction in this area for months. During this same time, I was also learning to give other things in my life to Him. I was going deeper and deeper into a relationship with Him, and He was opening my eyes to things I needed to take out of my life so that we could be closer. It wasn't until I had taken all distractions from my life and constantly renewed my mind in Him daily that I started to understand how this closeness with Him, which everyone can experience, really felt.

We must desire to be close with God, and I don't mean a halfhearted desire. I mean an all-out, nothing-held-back desire for closeness. We must choose Him instead of many other things that we could have or do. If we are not willing to fully commit to giving up everything for the heart of God, we will end up feeling alone. We will become frustrated because we "did a lot to gain His heart," yet we don't feel Him in our lives. If this is the case, something in our lives is still not fully surrendered to Him—and it needs to be pulled out by the roots. This process is not without some pain, but it is a most worthy one. "To all who mourn in Israel, he will give a crown of beauty for ashes, a joyous blessing instead of mourning, festive praise instead of despair. In their righteousness, they will be like great oaks that the Lord has planted for his own glory" (Isaiah 61:3 NLT).

I can say from experience that God is beautiful, and He is more than enough. I still have moments of feeling alone, but when they come, I go back to Him and renew my mind again in His love and presence, which comes in many actionable forms. This renewing is a daily necessity, if not a multiple-times-a-day necessity. As C. S. Lewis said, "Relying on God has to begin all over again every day as if nothing had yet been done."[3]

Even if we get married someday—and based on statistics, most of us will—*now* is the time to work on our relationship with God. We shouldn't wait until our husband comes along, because this is much more challenging when we have a person on whom to fall back. Our need won't be felt as acutely then, so we will have a tendency to put off actually coming to this place with Jesus. Our relationship with Christ, and loving Him in word and deed, is the most important thing in this world. But if we do not allow God to deal with us in this area of our lives, and we always allow someone to numb this void in us where God should be our all, most likely our ability to know Him fully will be hindered.

Paul encouraged people not to get married if they could control their sexual desires, because he understood that unmarried people are better able to completely devote their lives and time to God, rather than feeling torn between their family's needs and God's desires. (See 1 Corinthians 32–35.) This verse used to really annoy me, but it now makes complete sense as I have gained a greater understanding of what Paul meant. (We will talk more about this later.)

God created the institution of marriage to be a blessing in our lives, but more important, to show us how our relationship with Him can be closer. And yet having any other person that close to us in life can make it more challenging for us to keep Jesus first.

This is our time to search for God and seek His heart with abandon—not as preparation for anyone else, but because He is worth knowing and already loves us with abandon.

---

[3] C. S. Lewis, *Letters of C. S. Lewis*, p. 395.

3

WHO ARE YOU?

For this reason I bow my knees before the Father,
from whom every family in heaven and on earth derives its name,
that He would grant you, according to the riches of His glory,
to be strengthened with power through His Spirit in the inner man,
so that Christ may dwell in your hearts through faith; and that you,
being rooted and grounded in love,
may be able to comprehend with all the saints
what is the breadth and length and height and depth,
and to know the love of Christ which surpasses knowledge,
that you may be filled up to all the fullness of God.
—Ephesians 3:14–19

Who are you? Who does the Bible say you are? For us to understand our importance, or even find our direction in life, we need to understand who God says we are. No matter who the world may tell us we are or aren't, we must look to God, our Father, Lord, King, and Lover, to see clearly through the lies thrown at us by the world. These lies will always try to cover the truth of who we are and where we stand—and we stand on holy ground.

We Were Sinners

"We have all sinned and fallen short of the glory of God" (Romans 3:23). Even after we are saved, we will continue to have ingrained habits which include lusting after this world. But as we are changed into Jesus's likeness, these lusts will have less and less control over us. First John 2:16–17 talks about this challenge: "Do not love the world nor the things in the world. If anyone loves the world, the love of the Father is not in him. For all that is in the world, the lust of the flesh and the lust of the eyes and the boastful pride of life, is not from the Father, but is from the world."

We have a propensity to justify, with a multitude of excuses, the wrong choices we make to numb our convictions about those choices. Sometimes our bad choices don't seem *too* bad to us. Let's say, for example, that I look at regular (not pornographic) photos of men online or in a magazine, and I find a man whose looks I really like. If I then choose to spend my time and thoughts on him, even for a few seconds, that might not seem blatantly wrong. But where is my heart going when I choose to appreciate the way this man looks? He might have a beautiful image, but does that grant me the right to think about his form? It is just too easy to transition from appreciation to lust. Some might consider this a *small* sin, but truly it is a first solid step toward something much more serious.

We want to gloss over our decisions by trying to make them "not a big deal," yet everything we do has importance. Whether or not we see immediately their importance, our choices all have weight. Everything we do, whether in action or thought, will either draw us into a deeper relationship with God or block us from knowing Him intimately. In Genesis, Eve ate and condemned herself to physical and spiritual death, and it is the same for us. She demonstrated pride by thinking she deserved more and lusted for something she didn't already have, and her actions affected the whole world.

Do we lie to get what we want? Do we get angry with someone for not doing things the way we want? Do we steal, cheat, hate, lust, gossip, or get drunk? Even Paul said that he didn't do what he wanted to do, but rather did what he didn't want to do (Romans 7:18–19). Even with the saving power of Jesus Christ, we still have to constantly *choose* to follow Him. He will forgive our sins, but our need for His forgiveness means we have sins that need forgiving. Through Eve's sin, we all have been condemned to death, even before we are born. (See Psalm 51.)

We live in a broken world, and it is hard to avoid being scarred by its effects. As women, we are told every day that we need to dress a certain way to look beautiful. We are told we should work hard to be thin, so that we will be considered attractive. We should be appalled by the sensuality portrayed so often on TV and the Internet, but it has become commonplace. We have become numb, desensitized to this world and its hazards. We allow ourselves to be involved in the same activities as everyone else does, even when we feel the nagging inside to abstain. We show the depths of our true sinful nature by *not* helping the world the way Christ would, thus falling right in line with the nonbelievers all around us.

Don't misunderstand me—I am no better than anyone else. I still struggle daily, sometimes minute by minute, not to live this way. However, through God's grace, my eyes have been opened to my weakness, and "when I am weak, then I am strong" (2 Corinthians 12:10). Christ has given me His grace and strength. Praise Jesus!

The Redeemed

If we humble ourselves, realize our need, and accept the saving grace of Jesus, then we are no longer sinners by nature. Our old sinful nature dies when we accept the lordship of Jesus in our lives. As Romans 6:11 says, "Even so consider yourselves to be dead to sin, but alive to God in Christ Jesus."

We have received redemption: a new life, a new nature, a new start, a completely clean driving record from God. Every one of our sins has been wiped away, thrown "as far as the east is from the west" (Psalm 103:12). In other words, God has thrown our sins into a black hole from which they cannot return. Under this new covenant, He does not remember our transgressions, but says, "Their sins and their lawless deeds I will remember no more" (Hebrews 10:17).

We have been forgiven for everything wrong we have ever done, and we can start fresh because of Jesus's sacrifice. The enemy will try to remind us of our transgressions and create doubt and condemnation in our hearts, to prevent us from coming openly and humbly to God. But Jesus has paid the cost of our sin, which is now covered by His unmerited grace. Oh, God is so good!

When we come to God and ask forgiveness every time we commit a sin, God sees only the blood of Christ when He looks at us, and only those covered in Christ's blood can stand before God in confidence. We shouldn't expect to suddenly live perfect lives or never make wrong decisions again. We will still be warring against sinful desires, and the things that previously seemed normal to us will still try to occupy our time and commandeer our thoughts. But if we come to Jesus, ask forgiveness for the things we have done wrongly, and choose the purity of a relationship with Him over anything we are currently doing that is not for Him, He will not only forgive us but also teach us how to live in the freedom of His life.

Choosing God over the things we have before us is not always easy, but He has made it possible through the cross. God is so much better than any habit we have previously cultivated or any sinful impulse we could ever possibly satisfy. We are not sinners, but we must still choose not to sin, and that includes falling back into old habits. It is no longer our character to sin, since we are new in Christ, but this does not mean we won't be tempted.

I want to share with you a struggle I had for years. Even though I was redeemed by God, this one area of my life kept me in bondage for years and prevented me from living a fully redeemed life. My struggle was in the area of condemnation. I constantly felt condemned for—well, it seemed like almost everything. I wasn't smart enough, pretty enough, thin enough, cool enough, funny enough, wise enough, good enough, and so on. My life was crippled, but in God there is no condemnation.

"There is now no condemnation for those who are in Christ Jesus" (Romans 8:1).

For years, I believed that I was solely at fault for those self-condemning thoughts, which I allowed to build until I also became depressed. I didn't understand that I needed to submit them to God, thereby keeping Satan from gaining any ground. Just as the scripture says, "We are taking every thought captive to the obedience of Christ" (2 Corinthians 10:5).

Everything that comes into our minds, whether a subject of deep meditation or just a fleeting thought, needs to come under the submission of Jesus Christ. Then, if it is not holy, it should be immediately rebuked in Jesus's name and submitted to Jesus's authority.

This has required me to really pay attention to what I am thinking. I've learned to visualize myself taking the thought in my hands, telling it out loud to leave in Jesus's name, and then surrendering it to the Lord. I ask Him to take it from me and help me to set my heart and thoughts wholly on Him. I then fill my mind with personal songs of worship or simply think about what He says in His Word.

For a long time, I realized neither the active part I had to play in this process nor that my wrong thoughts and desires were not all my own. Some had been planted there by Satan, but after I heard them over and over again, I had accepted them as my own thoughts. I did not realize that he had not only deceived me into a wrong way of thinking, but also deceived me about where my thoughts came from. Satan hates God and the Holy Spirit who lives in me, and he will do anything to hurt God, including hurting me.

A few years ago, God gave me amazing understanding in this area, and I started to see the true power of Jesus's name. Learning about Him and walking in the freedom He gives is life changing. Through this whole process, I gained a better understanding of my depression and how complete freedom in Christ can look. (We will discuss this in a later chapter.)

However, to truly be able to walk in His freedom on a constant basis, we have to learn some things. For instance, if we return to the way we lived before surrendering to Christ, we grant Satan opportunities to torment us with the thoughts and desires we had given over to God. Satan is looking for every opportunity to destroy our lives. (See John 10:10.) When we watch or dwell mentally on ungodly things, we give Satan and his helpers an opening to come in and wreak havoc in our hearts and lives. We are constantly choosing between God and His holiness or something other, whether it be ourselves, other people, or the world around us. Whenever we choose anything other than God, we grant the enemy authority over parts of our lives—and he will try to use that authority to destroy us.

If you think this sounds intense, you're right. I can attest to this personally, with the things I allowed myself to watch or think about. I would pray, "Lord, why do I still have these thoughts that I had given to You?" And He clearly said, "Because you returned to your vomit, thereby giving the enemy an opening to torment you. You have to constantly bring Me your thoughts and not give Satan an opening. Your life must be holy and set apart." When I started doing this in all areas of my life, I began to understand the freedom and power that Jesus's name holds. Having made the decision to live a life set apart, as God has called all of us to do, I am trying to avoid influences in my life that could prevent me from hearing His voice, because there is nothing like really walking with the Lord. (See 1 Peter 1:14–16.)

A Daughter

The scriptures tell us God calls us His daughters under the new covenant through Jesus. "'I will dwell in them and walk among them; and I will be their God, and they shall be My people. Therefore, come out from their midst and be separate,' says the Lord. 'And do not touch what is unclean; and I will welcome you. I will be a father to you, and you shall be sons and daughters to Me,' says the Lord Almighty" (2 Corinthians 6:16–18).

God says He will dwell in us and be a father to us if we "come out from their midst." We need to stop surrounding ourselves with unholy influences and acting like people who are not children of God. We need to "be separate"—set apart for God—and obey his commandment to "not touch what is unclean." Then we are able to really experience this father-daughter relationship, in which we live together closely and learn how to live as daughters of the King.

As daughters of the King, we are true princesses, not fairy-tale princesses. Jesus tells us to pray, "Your Kingdom come" (Matthew 6:10). This present world is not our permanent kingdom, but only a foreshadowing of the kingdom in which we will dwell when Jesus comes again. Because this world is so corrupt, we do not see the evidence of our heritage daily, as we would if this world was in its perfected form. But if we understood that we are princesses in preparation for our reign in Christ's kingdom, would we not see ourselves differently? (See 2 Timothy 2:12.) Would we not see our responsibility and the importance of the time we have now? As children of God, we walk in His authority, but first we must understand what it means to be a daughter of the King.

This waiting period in which we are living is not a time to be stagnant, nor should we allow the world to define the waiting period for us. Normally we think of waiting as a time for doing nothing, as if we were standing in a long line of people with no end in sight, hoping something will eventually happen. No! This is a time for training and developing our character in Christ. We should be spending our days learning how to love Christ—and through loving Him, loving others as Christ loves us, which is no easy feat. We are to be "imitators of God" by showing His love to others (Ephesians 5:1). Paul says, "While we were yet sinners, Christ died for us" (Romans 5:8).

We are called to learn to love broken people in this broken world. This is a major part of being a daughter of the King, because He is love. Jesus walked among us to show us how to love the world. Just as He didn't wait to give us His love, we can't wait until people are more deserving of our love. We need to start loving them now, even while they are filthy with sin. This is a huge challenge. How easy is it to go up to a person on the street whose outward appearance is filthy and show them love? Or to show unconditional love to someone who is constantly tearing us down? Nevertheless, as His daughters, we are to extend the hand of our Father to those around us. We need to keep in mind that, unless God opens other people's eyes, it won't be possible for them to even see themselves the way God does. Sometimes He will choose to use us to help open their eyes, and often this is done by living out the love of Christ. (See John 13:34–35.) But to do this well, we must first be in a place where we understand the love God has for us.

As a princess is growing, is she locked in an isolated room in the palace? Of course not. She must be taught how to conduct herself with poise and grace. She needs to spend a decent amount of time alone with teachers and counselors, learning how she should live in the world, just as we do. But she also has lessons on how to live in a way that is befitting a daughter of the king. A princess is held to a higher standard than other people, because whatever she does reflects the power, authority, and character of her father. She is ultimately tied to her father, and everything she does will reflect either badly on the king or show his glory.

As daughters of the King, we are held to this same high standard. Everything we do reflects either well or poorly on our Father. Our actions don't actually change His character, but they will change the way that other people perceive Him. If we look at our history as Christians, we see that many people have formed opinions of our Father based on how others have acted.

I know people who choose not to believe in God, because their opinions about Him are based on the experiences they have had with Christians. They've told me that they think the concept of God is ridiculous because their Christian friend "is so legalistic and tells me all the wrong things I do." Or they tell me stories about how a pastor hurt them, or that they can't trust a specific Christian friend of theirs who always lies to them.

Everyone makes their own decision about whether to believe in Jesus, but still we must be careful about how we represent our Father to them. We can and should be working to prepare for kingdom life right now, rather than wasting our days sitting idle and looking to a future that is not here yet. We should use our days wisely and seek the Holy Spirit's guidance to know how to conduct ourselves as children of the King.

We should also keep something else in mind. It is beneath us to allow the men with whom we choose to be in relationships to use us or treat us in an unholy way. *We are daughters of the King,* and we should not settle for relationships in which we are neglected or abused— verbally, physically, or sexually. God does not intend for us to be torn down by words or looked at as sexual play toys, and He hurts for us when that happens.

We are beautiful and wonderfully made, and we are heirs with Christ. (See Psalm 139:14 and Romans 8:17.) We need to be careful to bind ourselves only to people who are seeking God wholeheartedly and who will call out this beauty in us. And when I say beauty, I do not mean sexuality. I mean the holy, pure beauty that Christ intends for His bride. We are worth this, and anything in us that says otherwise is from Satan. (In a later chapter, we'll discuss how to handle these thoughts.)

A Royal Priesthood

When we were born into the family of God, we were also given the honor of becoming part of the royal priesthood. (See 1 Peter 2:9.) As such, we are to conduct ourselves at all times in a fashion that brings honor to our Lord. The priests in the Old Testament had specific jobs and were daily required to burn sacrifices and bring offerings to

God, among other jobs. God chose them as His own, and they were required to live their lives set apart for Him. They were not given an inheritance of land, as were the other tribes of Israel when they took the Promised Land. Instead, God gave them Himself as their inheritance. (See Deuteronomy 18:2.)

Under the new covenant through Jesus, everyone who has given their lives to Christ is included in the royal priesthood. (See 1 Peter 2:9.) In 1 Peter 1:14–16, Peter says, "As obedient children, do not be conformed to the former lusts which were yours in your ignorance, but like the Holy One who called you, be holy yourselves also in all your behavior; because it is written, 'You shall be holy, for I am holy.'" It's hard to fully comprehend the magnitude of this concept, and I'm still working on it.

Although the specific practices of sacrificing animals and burning grain for God are things of the past, the spirit of such actions lives today. Instead of sacrificing animals, however, we are to sacrifice our lives to God. Romans 12:1 says we are "to present [our] bodies a living and holy sacrifice, acceptable to God which is [our] spiritual service of worship."

First, when Christ died His sacrifice made it so we could be holy. Second, our bodies and lives are to be treated as holy, meaning we should take care of them and be careful what we do with them. God does not accept offerings that are sick or broken, as seen in Malachi 1:8. Therefore, realizing our bodies should be a holy sacrifice to God, we need to learn what this means for us. The next part of this scripture in Romans twelve says that when we bring ourselves as a holy sacrifice to God, we are worshipping Him. Our lives can be lived in a way that worships the God who made us.

Jesus has already atoned for our transgressions, when He hung on the cross and bore our shame at Calvary. Since He paid the ultimate price for us, we can be certain of the forgiveness of our sins. However, Jesus said that if we want to follow Him, we have to pick up our own crosses every day. (See Luke 9:23.) We are to die every day to what we previously wanted in our lives. Instead, now we are to live as Christ did, living in submission to the Father. As Dietrich Bonhoeffer said, "When Christ calls a man, He bids him come and die."[4] In our daily lives, we should constantly remind ourselves and others about what Christ already did for us. Dying to ourselves is important, because that is part of how we demonstrate to the world our set-apart lives for Christ.

Old Testament priests were supposed to keep themselves clean, so that they could perform their priestly duties. Before they could enter the temple, they had to complete cleansing rituals to make sure they did not carry any filth, including sin, into the inner part of the temple with them. As priests today, we bring our lives as daily offerings to God, whether or not we comprehend this. By accepting Christ's gift of grace, we have also agreed to live for Him. Our days now belong to Him, so everything we do is a sacrifice, whether holy or filthy.

I am not saying this to bring condemnation, but to bring understanding to the weight of our daily decisions. God knows we are still struggling with sinful desires, but He is always there, ready to help us repent and turn from our sin, thus moving closer to Him. We should be on alert for things that might cause us to sin and rob us of a close relationship with God. A close relationship with God requires that we constantly work toward setting every detail of our lives apart for Him. We will not be able to pick and choose what things or people in our lives we want to give to God—everything must be surrendered. If we are doing anything that isn't purely for God, we should take the time to evaluate our true motives for doing it.

I don't mean to encourage legalism, which is just as far away from the heart of God as blatant sin, as seen by the lives of the Pharisees. But I hope that we see how all-encompassing God's involvement and influence should be in our lives. To live God's way, we need Him to help us in every area of our lives. We do not have the strength or desire for a pure life, apart from God and the prompting of His Spirit.

Maybe some of us don't really want to be priests. But if we have accepted the grace of Jesus and given our lives to Him, then we have

---

[4] Dietrich Bonhoeffer, *The Cost of Discipleship*, p. 89.

been entrusted with this gift. As priests, we have two choices—to conduct ourselves honorably or to lead filthy lives and attempt to keep parts of our lives for ourselves. If we choose the latter, we'll never really know God, His love, and His full purpose for our lives. Every individual part of our lives affects every other part of our lives. We will desire more of whatever we dwell on or spend time on, whether it be God or the world. (See Matthew 6:21.)

However, the choice is yours. I pray that you will choose to dedicate your whole life to God and not keep any part to yourself. I encourage you to not wait until your life is comfortable before choosing to make God's life more important than your own. Honestly, if we reach a comfortable stage in life, we're less likely to choose to give that up for God. If we've avoided choosing God until then, what really makes us think that will change when we are leading lives of worldly comfort?

A Servant

Just before Christ was taken to the cross, how did He use His time? He did not use it to teach us how to be rich or powerful, nor did He teach us how to take the world by force. Instead He washed His disciples' feet, to teach us how to be servants to others. During Passover, the disciples quarreled about who would be greatest in the kingdom of God, but Jesus drew them back to the importance of being a servant. "And He said to them, 'The Kings of the Gentiles lord it over them; and those who have authority over them are called *Benefactors*. But it is not this way with you, but the one who is the greatest among you must become like the youngest, and the leader like the servant. For who is greater, the one who reclines at the table or the one who serves? Is it not the one who reclines at the table? But I am among you as the one who serves'" (Luke 22:25–27).

Jesus's entire ministry was a demonstration of how to be a servant. He was available to people in need, whether He was tired or not. In fact,

I suspect that He never had much time to sleep. I like sleep—*a lot*—but lately I've realized how often Jesus rose early to pray. That seemed to be His best opportunity to spend alone time with His Father, so that He knew what His Father was doing in heaven. Jesus was constantly in communion with the Father through the Holy Spirit, but His early mornings alone with God where He invested in their relationship gave Him the strength to love others and serve them wholeheartedly.

Jesus was fully God, but He was also fully man. People and things in His life tried to pull Him away and distract Him from His Father's heart, but He understood the importance of taking time to focus on His relationship with His Father. The strength and focus we gain in our personal times with Him will help other people see Christ in us. As tough as it may sound, sometimes we need communion with Him more than we need sleep.

How much humility does it take to allow people to see who we are and then allow them, if they choose, to make fun of us or even shut us out completely? The confidence to do this comes only from Christ, the only true security we will ever have in life. If we can come to the place of being His servant to others, and allow others to reject us if they choose to do so, He will use us in ways unfathomable.

This is a hard lesson for some of us to learn. I have never liked being rejected. Really, who does? I first remember experiencing rejection as a child of about eight. That rejection lasted for years and scarred me deeply, and I am surprised at times by how much it still affects my life today. For years, I rarely showed anyone the real me, for fear of being rejected again. It has been many years since I forgave the people who hurt me, and God has helped me love them despite what they did, but because of this rejection I still sometimes find it difficult to trust.

But Jesus, who had no good reason to be rejected, was rejected so strongly that He was crucified while we looked on and mocked Him. He loved so much that He allowed us to humiliate and kill Him. By serving others, we get to show them and even ourselves the heart of God, who loved unto death and calls us to do the same. He says in

Revelation that those who will overcome will be those who "did not love their life even when faced with death" (Revelation 12:11). We must be willing to serve Jesus with our lives, no matter the cost.

An Heir

The scriptures call Jesus the *firstborn*, signifying that others were to come after Him. (See Colossians 1:15.) "The Spirit Himself testifies with our spirit that we are children of God, and if children, heirs also, heirs of God and fellow heirs with Christ, if indeed we suffer with Him so that we may also be glorified with Him" (Romans 8:16–17). We are now brothers and sisters to Christ, children of God. As such, we are recipients of the love and affection that all children are supposed to get from their parents.

We also have been given the right to live in the authority of a son or daughter of God. Now, this is rather weighty. I don't think most people understand it, and I myself am still trying to understand it. Now that we are born again into the family of Christ, as daughters of God, we have inherited the authority of God as part of our birthright. We don't do anything to earn it. Instead, it is part of our inheritance when we accept Christ's sacrifice for us.

Being given authority through Christ doesn't mean we know how to live with this authority. Just as with our earthly parents, when we live in a trustworthy manner, God grants us more freedom to use the authority that He has given to us. As we grow and learn to live out Christ's character, God will increase our level of authority and responsibility, because He sees we can handle it well. The authority of Christ is ours, but He will allow us to walk in it only as we grow in Him. He protects us by doing this in stages as we grow. God wants us to learn how to use the authority He has given us in the places we are now, and as we grow in these areas, He will open up more ways for us to walk in more of His authority.

In most of the world, including first-world countries and modern Western societies, women and daughters unfortunately do not have the same rights or authority as men. This is part of the curse placed on women in the garden of Eden after the "fall of man." (*Man* is used here in the generic sense to include both men and women.) God said to Eve, "He will rule over you" (Genesis 3:16).

Just because the world has seen the effects of, and is still dealing with, this curse doesn't mean this is how the world was initially designed. If Adam had ruled over Eve from the beginning, there would have been no purpose for this curse. Likewise, in the scriptural story about the creation of Eve, Adam says he could not find any other creature who was his kind. So God created him a partner, someone to work alongside him—not under him or subservient to him, but a partner, a helpmate. Matthew Henry describes this beautifully in *An Exposition of the Old and New Testaments*: "The woman was made of a rib out of the side of Adam; not made out of his head to top him, not out of his feet to be trampled upon by him, but out of his side to be equal with him, under his arm to be protected, and near his heart to be beloved."[5]

This gives us a glimpse of how we are meant to be, co-heirs with men through Christ Jesus. After we are saved, we are given the same authority as men—no more and no less—through Jesus from the Father. This has nothing to do with the world's concept of women's rights. We have been given Christ's authority, which is beyond our comprehension here, but we are also to live in submission to Him and other people whom God has placed in authority over us, and often there will be a man in authority over us. God shows us how to live in submission, and because we walk in this submission to Him and those over us, we are better able to use His authority appropriately. Everything in God is balanced and works together perfectly, even though it's hard for us to fully live this way while living in a broken world.

Because of the amazing love of God, we are given a position in heaven like that of Jesus. In Revelation 3:21, Jesus says, "He who

[5] Matthew Henry, *An Exposition of the Old and New Testaments*, p. 36.

overcomes, I will grant him to sit down with Me on My throne, as I also overcame and sat down with My Father on His throne." Wow, I can't even wrap my head around this. Because of Jesus's sacrifice and my willingness to follow His guidance throughout my life, He will give me this place of honor, which comes with responsibility and authority through Christ. This is truly humbling.

But we must not forget the end of verse 17 in Romans, where Paul says we have been made "fellow heirs with Christ, if indeed we suffer with Him so that we may also be glorified with Him" (Romans 8:17). We can't live in the authority of Christ properly unless we live and die for Jesus and His glory. We must be willing to suffer for Christ, not shy away from the world's disapproval and hatred. We shouldn't run into danger blindly, but we need to have our eyes focused on Christ and follow wherever He leads—no matter the outcome. This is where our true power in Christ comes from, and where we will start to live as an heir with Christ.

A Testimony

Our whole lives should be a testimony to who God is. Everything we do, say, and think should point to Jesus, who saved us. Revelation 12:11 says, "And they overcame him because of the blood of the Lamb and because of the word of their testimony, and they did not love their life even when faced with death." We are "they," and our lives are this testimony, which is part of the way we overcome Satan. Christ has already given His part—His blood—but we must learn to love Jesus more than we love our own lives, even unto death.

Even though dying for Christ sounds like an extremely difficult thing, over the years I've reached the conclusion that genuinely living for Christ is even harder. Living for Christ requires a daily commitment, which is a challenge but is also where His power lies. It is in the daily grind of life that He wants to meet us and work through us, and where

He wants us to help others meet Him. We just have to be open to Him and willing to be that testimony. We are constantly giving testimony to who God is and what He is like, whether we realize it or not. The power of Christ is at work in our lives in helping us overcome Satan day by day, through Christ's blood and our testimony.

Our thoughts, words, and actions—as well as the way we use our time, money, and other resources—are all part of our testimony. I don't say these things to add an unneeded burden but to speak the truth. We can't do God's will, not even for a moment, without Jesus helping us and making it possible. Jesus doesn't give us freedom *from* these things, but He does free us to truly live well.

A Bride

In the Song of Solomon, we are called *beloved*. In Revelation, we are identified as the bride of Christ, clothed in white. The Bible tells us that a man is to love his wife as Christ loves His bride, which is the church, and the bride is to obey her husband like the church is to obey Christ. (See Ephesians 5:22-29.) Everything God set in motion from the foundation of the world is supposed to make us aware of our need for Him and reveal His love for us. The relationship between a husband and wife is the most intimate one we see on this earth, and yet it doesn't begin to compare with the relationship God longs to have with us.

"'It will come about in that day,' declares the Lord, 'That you will call Me Ishi and will no longer call Me Baali. For I will remove the names of the Baals from her mouth, so that they will be mentioned by their names no more ... I will betroth you to Me forever; Yes, I will betroth you to Me in righteousness and in justice, in loving-kindness and in compassion, and I will betroth you to Me in faithfulness. Then you will know the Lord'" (Hosea 2:16–17,19–20).

Let's try to understand this scripture. First, the word *Ishi* means "my husband" and *Baali* means "my master." God is saying He no longer wants us to know Him as our master, but instead as our husband. He no longer wants our relationship with Him to be like that of a master and slave, but like that of a husband and wife instead. God will betroth us to Him just as a husband does with the woman whom he is to marry. But God does this in complete and pure righteousness, justice, loving-kindness, compassion, and faithfulness.

This deep, loving relationship with God will eliminate our desire for our former ways of living. The reason we previously worshipped the things we did was that they occupied our hearts and took up our time, whether money, beauty, physical fitness, movies, TV, people, and so on. But now, because of God's love in our lives, these things mean little to us anymore. Their importance in our lives is moderated by a more realistic sense of their true value. When we have a deep, intimate relationship with God, that only deepens our desire to live for Him and serve others.

Engaging in a husband-and-wife type of intimate relationship with Christ may seem odd if we think of it in sexual terms. And yet the act of sexual intercourse is the best example God gave of the closeness God wants with us, but that's not how Christ will spend intimate time with us.

Some of my experiences with Christ, through the Holy Spirit, who lives within me, have helped me understand the deep, pervasive, intimate desire that God has for us and how He expresses this. Some of my most intimate times with the Holy Spirit have left me in a state of euphoria, when my whole being feels alive and almost buzzing. Because He dwells inside me, and His life and love come with Him, my body has a hard time containing the experience of His presence at times. He desires that we live in a way that invites Him into the intimate parts of who we are. Here and now, He is the light of our days and the One with whom we look forward to living.

But we must keep in mind that, as it says in Revelation, we are to clothe ourselves in the white garment of His bride. God gives this garment to us through salvation, but *we* have to choose to put it on. "It was given to her to *clothe herself* in fine linen, bright and clean: for the fine linen is the righteous acts of the saints" (Revelation 19:8; emphasis added).

We are all born sinful, but He chose to give us His righteousness because He loves us. But first we must choose to clothe ourselves in the "fine linen" that represents these righteous acts throughout our lives. We can't wait until Jesus returns, because then it will be too late, and we will be brides scantily clad and wholly unprepared for our weddings.

In Matthew, Jesus tells the story of a wedding where one of the guests was not properly dressed because he had not put on the righteous acts of Christ. "When the king came in to look over the dinner guests, he saw a man there who was not dressed in wedding clothes, and he said to him, 'Friend, how did you come in here without wedding clothes?' and the man was speechless. Then the king said to the servants, 'Bind him hand and foot, and throw him into the outer darkness; in that place there will be weeping and gnashing of teeth" (Matthew 22:11–13).

Jesus says that if we have not properly dressed ourselves in the righteous acts He has given us, God will have us thrown out of the wedding between Christ and His bride. We must not let our lives slip by without seeing the need for living in the righteous acts of Christ. With true salvation comes true repentance, and with repentance comes a changing of our ways. We will no longer desire the former things, but will begin to desire the righteousness of God. For as we come to see Him more clearly, we will be made more like Him. (See 1 John 3:2.) Let us not forget the importance of putting on the robes of righteousness every day.

4

WHOM DO YOU SERVE?

For from Him and through Him and to Him
are all things. To Him be the glory forever. Amen.

—Romans 11:36

I would hope the question "Whom do you serve?" could be easily answered by any Christian, but in this world it can be complicated. We have allowed our eyes to be blinded by many things, and in many areas we have been lulled into complacency. In Revelation 3:16, God is talking to a church when He says, "Because you are lukewarm, and neither hot nor cold, I will spit you out of My mouth." I fear the word *lukewarm* is descriptive of too many people who claim to be Christian in today's Western culture.

I myself was complacent for years, and many areas in my life still need work. Having recognized my condition, though, I do not want to stay where I am, because the last thing I want is to be spit out of God's mouth. That would be a good sign that our Christian lives haven't measured up to what God wanted from us.

The next verse in Revelation aptly describes the culture in this generation which wants to work its way undetected into the church: "Because you say, 'I am rich, and have become wealthy, and have need of nothing,' and you do not know that you are wretched and miserable and poor and blind and naked" (Revelation 3:17). For many of us, our physical wants and needs have been met, but we don't perceive our own spiritual need. We want more and more stuff to fill the void inside us, a void that nothing and no one can fill but God. Try as we might, all the things for which we strive just give us a larger appetite for a menagerie of things we don't really need. In the long run, trying to satisfy our appetites with worldly things makes us numb and despondent, because they provide us with no satisfaction, no matter how hard we try. Everything we seek, outside of God, leaves us empty.

If we don't listen to our dissatisfied and empty hearts, then we become the dreaded *lukewarm* mentioned in Revelation 3:16. It's when we feel this emptiness that many of us finally realize our true situation and choose to do something about it. Others people settle for the numbing nothingness that being lukewarm brings, even though no one gains anything from being lukewarm. Are we hot or cold toward God? For years, my attitude was, "How little can I do for God and still be blessed?" To be honest, I wasn't living for God. I was living for myself under the guise of living "a good Christian life."

If we had to stand before the Lord today and give an account of how we are living our lives right now, could we honestly say we are living for Him? What would be our proof? Do our lives *show* that we are living for God?

Daily Living

Before we get too far into this subject of living daily for God, I want to share an understanding that God has been working in me, although it has taken me a while to learn it. When we are learning something new, we often need rules and principles to keep us going in the right direction. Like in music, we need rules of time signatures and major and minor melodies to shape our foundation. Yet, once we have learned the rules, principles, guidelines then we eventually can step outside the established boundaries and take liberties that we were not able to take earlier. Of course, God's Word *never* changes, and we are not to try to change that. But we can often make our own choices with regard to the decisions that affect our daily lives.

Sometimes God wants us to talk with specific people, or take on certain jobs, or purchase particular homes. At other times, however, He will honor whatever decisions we make. God created each of us with our own likes, dislikes, desires, and passions, and He wants us to be true to ourselves and make our own choices. Sometimes freedom of choice follows a season during which we learn what the heart of God really wants. Then God sets us loose to see what we have learned and whether that has an effect on how we choose to live. But at other times, God simply says, "It's your choice. What do you want?"

God delights in seeing us grow and watching our lives become full and joyous. He wants us to be the owners of our own lives. We should always seek the will of God for our daily lives and ask his guidance in the choices we make, but sometimes God's will is just for us to be ourselves. God desires for us to live for Him, but there isn't necessarily any contradiction between living for Him and choosing something that we really desire. Actually, as we grow in Him, those two things will contradict each other less often.

With this understanding in place, let's return to our foundational understanding of daily living for God, because we often need to learn the rules and guidelines before we can really walk in freedom.

How do we spend our time during the day? In the past, on a good day I might read my Bible and pray, but then I'd be free to do whatever I wanted for the rest of the day, unless I had to attend to work or school. My relationship with Jesus had not always been like that. But gradually, because of my lack of intentionality or understanding, along with disappointments from wrongfully placed expectations, my desire for Him had become distanced and clouded. Eventually I read the Bible and prayed only because it was what I was supposed to do, not because my heart was in it.

Back then, my primary motivation was selfish ambition, because I wanted God to give me what I wanted in life. But God doesn't give us new life so that we can just live for ourselves. Our lives should be given to God just as much as Jesus's life was given for us. "I have been crucified with Christ; and it is no longer I who live, but Christ lives in me" (Galatians 2:20). When I accepted Christ's salvation, I gave Him full rights to every aspect of my life, of which He is now the author and lord. In return, I am given His forgiveness, grace, and redemption, among many other blessings.

We all find ways to fill our days, but are we using our time wisely? Most people would say, "Oh, I don't have to be productive with *every* moment of my day." But is that how God looks at our lives? Is He thinking, *They just want to use part of their lives for Me, and that's okay. I don't really want them to give Me everything they have.* Or does He desire for us to use every moment of every day to bring glory to His name and show others the reason for Jesus's sacrifice on the cross? Are we being good stewards of the gifts that have been given to us through His sacrifice?

God has been talking to me about purpose and the importance of being intentional in everything I do. No laziness is allowed, which is a difficult challenge. We might think, *I can* never *be lazy. I'm not sure I can give that much of me.* Well, then what *are* we sure of? If we have given our lives to God and accepted Jesus as our Lord and Savior, then we know that He came so that we "may have life and have it abundantly" (John 10:10). But we shouldn't think that we are free to do as we please with our new lives. We may choose to squander our lives and do whatever we want, but there are consequences to every choice we make. According to scripture, *everyone* will be judged, not just those who do not believe in Jesus as Lord. When Peter says, "It is time for judgment to begin with the household of God" (1 Peter 4:17), he is talking to the church, not to unbelievers.

We are to obey God's Word, which tells us many things: love the Lord, love one another, give to others, lay down our lives one for another, and so on. The most important of these is to love the Lord our God with all our heart. And if we *do* love God with all our heart, then the other things we are told to do in the Bible should come from an overflow of our love for Him. Our love for God is the foundation on which every aspect of our lives should be built. It is only through our love for Him that we will *want* to live every moment for Him. God knows that sometimes we need to rest and just be still, but He can use even our stillness to grow us in amazing ways. He wants us to experience everything He has in store for us, both here *and* in eternity. (See Psalm 103:14, 139:16.) He doesn't want us to miss out on a single part of His joy, which we can have now. God wants to use every moment of every day to reach us with His presence, and that can happen if we allow Him.

Christians are taught that Jesus's blood covers all sins, which is true. However, we must also pay attention to the first part of this verse, which says, "But if we walk in the Light as He Himself is in the Light, we have fellowship with one another, and the blood of Jesus His Son cleanses us from all sin" (1 John 1:7). This verse makes an if/then statement; if we actively live in the Light of Christ, then His blood will cleanse us.

As we love God, we will develop the desire to live for Him in obedience, and the Bible provides us with guidelines for how to do that. In the gospel of John, we have an example of how loving God will make us want to obey Him. Jesus says to Simon, "'Simon, son of John, do you love Me?' He said to him, 'Yes, Lord; You know that I love You.' He said to him, 'Shepherd My sheep'" (John 21:16). Jesus said this three times to Simon, which not only helped Him get to the root of Simon's denial of Jesus three times on the night He was betrayed, but also reinforces the importance of learning this about the heart of God. God wants us to love Him, and as a result of that love, we will care for, help, love, and teach His other children.

Though we are weak and imperfect, time and again He forgives our failures, just as He did for Simon when he denied Christ three times. However, we must not treat His redemption with flippancy. If we use His salvation to justify living however we desire, and we don't repent and obey Him, we have only fooled ourselves with a false salvation that cannot redeem our broken lives. John the Baptist says in John 3:36, "He who believes in the Son has eternal life; but he who does not *obey* the Son will not see life, but the wrath of God abides on him" (emphasis added).

Truly loving Christ creates a desire within us to obey Him and surrender our lives to Him. Our desire for Jesus will create in us a passion so strong that we would lay down our lives for Him, just as He did for us. And how else do we accomplish this, except to daily live for Him, rather than for ourselves?

It is difficult for us to desire to love someone whom we do not know well and might not even trust, let alone to love Him more than we love ourselves. The scriptures tell us about Christ's faithfulness and kindness, but it is another matter entirely to understand these wonders through experience. That's why it is so important to spend time alone with Him, talk with Him in prayer, and read His Word every day. I pray that our hearts may be opened to the deep, wide, and all-consuming love of Christ. Until we can begin to comprehend the depths of His love toward us, it's almost impossible to desire to live our lives completely for Him.

As a teenager, I would read the Bible and think to myself, *If I was given the choice to deny Christ and live or claim Christ as Lord and die, would I make the right decision?* As I have gotten older, living for Him seems harder than dying for Him would be. Living for Christ requires a constant commitment to love Him more than I love myself and to desire Him above all other things in my life.

To live this life that has been given to me well, I am not to look for my own gain, but for the benefit that Christ will receive through how I live for Him. Jesus left us here to fulfill a purpose—to have a relationship with God—and the Holy Spirit wants to work toward this purpose in our lives. As a result of our relationship with God, we learn how to be more like Christ and we delight in sharing His love with other people.

In John 17:15, Jesus says to His Father, "I do not ask You to take them out of the world, but to keep them from the evil one." He didn't take the disciples away with Him because they still had a purpose here on earth, just as we do now. Satan, the "evil one," wants to meddle in our lives—to steal, kill, and destroy the lives that we are meant to live for the Lord. (See John 10:10.) That is just what Satan does, mostly

47

through deceiving us. On a daily basis, the enemy lies to us in such small and inconspicuous ways that we have a tendency not to notice them anymore.

One way the modern church has been deceived is in its lack of reverence for God, a concept that we no longer really understand. This irreverence has been intensifying slowly over the last few generations, which makes it the deadliest form of deception. People treat God with unabashed flippancy and take license to do whatever they want with His grace, offering the excuse that they are doing so "for God." The Bible tells us that we will be known by our fruits. If our heart is focused on what we want from God, it will show in what we are physically pursuing. Unfortunately, sometimes when we have allowed ourselves to be deeply deceived, it can take a while for the focus of our hearts to surface. But if our hearts are set on God alone, that will be evident in our lives, "and all these things will be added to you" (Matthew 6:33). God provides us with Himself and everything we could ever need.

What do we desire? Are we truly seeking the heart of God, or are we seeking God for our own selfish purposes? God *loves* answering our prayers, but He wants our prayers to be focused on Him and nothing else. God loves it when we talk with Him, and He wants to be intimately involved with our daily lives. He desires to help us with everything, whether large or small, because He loves being our Father.

Unfortunately, when we seek direction from God, most of us act like Balaam. We ask God a question, but when we don't like the answer, we keep asking Him, hoping His answer will change. And when He finally lets us go in the direction we want, even after He warned us not to do so, what happens? The way is hard and the path is painful, so we complain to Him about how difficult it is. God will never take away our free will and *force* us to go a particular way. He will always allow us to choose, but we should be careful about choosing something that God has advised us against.

The challenge in these times can be likened to the donkey in the story of Balaam. These challenges are trying to keep us from meeting an untimely end because we were coveting something God didn't want for us in the first place.

Balaam

You may be asking, "Who is Balaam, and why is she talking about a donkey?" Balaam was a prophet, and the people of his time knew that Balaam had a relationship with God and spoke the word of God. (See Numbers 22.) People would go to Balaam to get a blessing from God. One day a king asked Balaam to curse the children of Israel. This king was scared of the Israelites and their power, so he wanted God to curse them. The only problem was that the king was asking God to curse His own people, which wasn't really a smart thing for the king to do.

When Balaam prayed for God's guidance, God told him not to curse the Israelites. So Balaam told the king, through the king's messengers, that God would not let him fulfill the king's request. The king decided he had not offered Balaam enough money, so he sent his messengers back to Balaam to sweeten the deal. Prophets during this time in history were often paid for the services they rendered, since that was their job. So Balaam again asked God if he could curse the Israelites, but this time God told Balaam that he could go with the messengers back to the king. God didn't say that Balaam could curse the Israelites, but only that he could go back with the king's messengers. But as soon as Balaam did that, God became angry and an angel appeared in Balaam's path and blocked him from proceeding.

The donkey that Balaam was riding tried to steer Balaam away from the angel, who was waiting to kill him. When the donkey took Balaam through a narrow place, Balaam's foot was smashed against a wall. Eventually, when the donkey realized there was no way to go forward on the narrow path that the angel was blocking, he lay down on the ground and refused to continue. Balaam was angry at his donkey the whole time and kept hitting him. Balaam did not realize, as the donkey did, that he was in danger of death. But then God let the donkey talk with the voice of a man to tell Balaam what was happening.

God had become angry when Balaam did not do what God told him to do in the first place. God did eventually tell Balaam he could go, but He did so only because Balaam kept pushing for a different answer. Because of his lack of holy fear and reverence, Balaam had kept pushing because he lusted for the riches and honor he could gain from the king. Balaam's eyes were not set on God, but on what he wanted to gain through the situation.

This story is a warning to us that what God says goes. We should not try—to the point of irreverence—to get God to change His answer. God understands when we come to Him humbly with questions about His will, but when we have been given an answer, we would be wise to accept it and honor His decision. God knows that we do not always want what He wants, and He knows it will often take us time to adjust our hearts and minds to His ways. His ways are much higher than our ways and we will not often understand them. (See Isaiah 55:9.) But He is patient with us, and we should praise Him for that! (See 2 Peter 3:9.) He is joyous when we choose Him and His desires over our own. Choosing God first will always help build our relationship with Him, and it is something we should strive to do daily.

God loves us so deeply, regardless of what we do or the choices we make. He always wants the best for us, whether or not we recognize this in the moment of desire. Reminding ourselves of God's deep love for us is key in these times. "So that Christ may dwell in your hearts through faith; and that you, being rooted and grounded in love, may be able to comprehend with all the saints what is the breadth and length and height and depth, and to know the love of Christ which surpasses knowledge, that you may be filled up to all the fullness of God" (Ephesians 3:17–19).

With Whom Are You Building?

We need to be careful that we're building on the right foundation, like the story in the gospel of Matthew about the difference between building on sand or rock. (See Matthew 7:24–27.) We can build our lives on a foundation of sand, such as the ideas and principles of the world, or on the rock foundation of the character and truth of Jesus. Also, our foundation can be affected by the teachings to which we listen, because our understanding of Jesus can be corrupted by outside influences. If we are taught principles that are not of God, even though we are told they are, our foundation might not be made entirely of who God is. We might end up with an uneven, cracked foundation because we have adopted wrong beliefs. This is why everything we hear and learn should be checked by scripture, which is God's Word, to verify its truth. We want lives that will stand, no matter what is happening, and only through a foundation of the truth of Jesus is this possible.

However, when our foundation is set, that doesn't mean we should then just accept any so-called "godly" teacher's guidance about how to build our spiritual house. In building an actual house, we shouldn't put up Sheetrock before the framing is in place, and the same principle works in our spiritual lives.

A few years ago, I helped my parents build their house. The framers put up the house's framework, including the two-by-four framing for the walls and the larger beams for the roof. If I stood in just the right place on one side of the house, I could see all the way through to the other side. I remember thinking then, *All right, let's get some Sheetrock up on this frame.* I had never built a house, and I didn't realize all the steps that needed to be taken before the Sheetrock went up, such as electrical wiring, insulation, and plumbing. Someone needed to go through the whole framed house and make sure all the wooden frame pieces were in the right places, not sticking out where they shouldn't, and even look for stray nails that needed to be removed. We also needed to make sure the framers actually put the walls where they were supposed to, and that the walls hadn't been erected in the wrong place.

If we had skipped any of these steps before putting Sheetrock on the frame, the house might not have ended up with electrical outlets that worked or doorways that fit normal-sized doors. It could have been really cold in the winter because of missing insulation, or the plumbing might not have been connected to the toilets and tubs. Sometimes parts of the framework had to be taken out and moved, because the framers hadn't followed the blueprints faithfully. I think back and remember how sometimes I wished we could *just get to the Sheetrock work already*. But I can only imagine how time consuming and frustrating it would have been if we had been forced to remove Sheetrock to fix what was underneath—just because we hadn't followed certain crucial steps first.

We should be equally careful in building our spiritual lives. The choices we make and how we go about executing those choices have consequences. Occasionally it is necessary to tear out part of a wall in our physical house to fix or improve something, and sometimes the same thing happens with our spiritual houses if we have built something that isn't working right or glorifying Him.

Anyone with whom we spend our lives will ultimately shape the direction we go in life. The closer another person is to us, the more influence they have over us. Because of this, if the people to whom we are close do not advocate matching everything to the Word of God, we should be cautious of their influence. Eventually we could either give in and not care how things line up with God's Word, or we could become one of those people who goes too far and twists God's Word into whatever is convenient at the time. Verse 9 in 2 John says, "Anyone who goes too far and does not abide in the teaching of Christ, does not have God; the one who abides in the teaching, he has both the Father and the Son."

God didn't give us His Word simply for convenience. It is truth and life, and we must respect it and always be careful to bring everything we do back to it. That includes being sensitive to how we allow other people to influence our decisions.

Many new Christians don't know—because they haven't been taught—about the process of building their spiritual lives. That's why so many people who have been Christians for a while still seem so weak in their faith, almost like infants. How are we to know that we need something if it isn't talked about? Instead, we end up thinking, *Oh, this person is a Christian and she probably knows more than me.* We build on what other people tell us, but we have not learned how to hold everything up to the light of God's Word to check for its truth. In the long run, we end up frustrated because we have been promised that life will be a certain way or that we will have certain things. But who made those promises to us, God or another person?

God has promised us abundant lives, but that does not mean that life will be without its challenges. (See John 10:10.) On the contrary, He promised us a life of trials. In John 16:33, Jesus says, "These things I have spoken to you, so that in Me you may have peace. In the world you have tribulation, but take courage; I have overcome the world."

Not only does Jesus make life possible, but He makes it possible for us to live an abundant life through Him, here and now. He will not only sustain us through the trials we face, but He has already overcome every trial. Praise God!

Take a minute and think through these next questions. You might have become saved a long time ago, but how is your house being built? Who is recommending building materials to you? Which teachers are you allowing to speak into your life? Are you being taught to base all of your beliefs on Jesus and His Word, or are you following the words of other people? Are you really aware of what the scriptures say? Are you choosing the word of someone else over the Word of God?

I do not say these things to bring discouragement, but to bring honesty and understanding from the heart of God. He wants to be loved, revered, and worshipped. He loves us more than we can comprehend, but it isn't a love that we should trample on or push aside whenever we want to do something of which He will not approve. We should expect there to be consequences to any choices that hurt our relationship with Him. The Holy Spirit is an incredible gift, but we can't pick and choose when and where He will be with us.

We must choose this day whom we will serve, ourselves or God. (See Colossians 3:25.) We cannot have His grace while living our lives in whatever way we choose. We can choose grace, which means also surrendering to His will. Or we can choose our own way, which means eventually being told by the bridegroom, Jesus, "I do not know you" (Matthew 25:12). Those five foolish virgins mentioned in the gospel of Matthew were not willing to give what was necessary and be faithful. In the end, even though they believed Jesus was coming back, their lack of preparation cost them more than they could have imagined.

In the next section, I will address a few major aspects of God and who He is. These are highlights from specific thoughts and understandings God is working in me still. May God's truth be strong in my weakness!

I AM

If we believe in God, why would we think that we have any rights? We are only the creation, not the Creator. Who is the clay, that it dares to question the potter? (See Isaiah 45:9.) Our pervasive feeling of pride and entitlement prompts us to question Him. God didn't have to make us heirs with Christ and give us an inheritance, but that is not who He is. He is an amazing God! He chose to give us these rights as His children, but too often we act like we deserve them. We're far too familiar and irreverent with God, but it was their irreverent familiarity with God that got Aaron's two sons killed. (See Leviticus 9:1–3.)

I have entered God's presence many times without the proper reverence. When I go to church, am I going in reverence—or do I go to church just like I go anywhere else? Of course, church is neither the only place where we encounter God nor the only place where we should show Him reverence. However, that's where I first noticed this lack of reverence. I would go to church thinking, *Today will be just like every other Sunday. I will greet friends, sing a few praise songs, listen to the pastor, talk with more friends, and then go home* ... Hey, wait a minute! Where is God in all this? His Spirit is present, but what is my focus?

We have become too comfortable with our expectations for church meetings—or even for what our daily "quiet time" with the Lord will look like. Because of this, we have lost a degree of reverence for the One whom we believe we are worshipping. We have come to expect so much from Him, but we don't give Him proper respect and reverence. We often live like spoiled children who do whatever they want in the presence of their parents, expecting no repercussions. We live in a time of grace, but that does not mean that the God of grace will forever withhold consequences or judgment. He is also our judge, and one day we will be judged for everything we have thought and done. We will have to live for eternity with the consequences of our choices. (See Romans 2:16, 2 Corinthians 5:10.)

God is not weak or sweet, but He is good and holy. His goodness, righteousness, and holiness work so tightly together that we can't have one without the others. His holiness will not let unrighteousness stand before Him. (See Psalm 1:5.) He will not allow His goodness to be watered down or reduced by unrighteousness, nor will He ever stray from His purity and holiness. God's goodness goes hand in hand with His mercy and judgment. In *The Knowledge of the Holy*, A. W. Tozer cautions us as follows:

> God's compassion flows out of His goodness, and goodness without justice is not goodness. God spares us because He is good, but He could not be good if He were not just ... The vague and tenuous hope that God is too kind to punish the ungodly has become a deadly opiate for the consciences of millions. It hushes their fears and allows them to practice all pleasant forms of iniquity while death draws every day nearer

and the command to repent goes unregarded. As responsible
moral beings we dare not so trifle with our eternal futures.[6]

God is a holy fire that demands us to be cleansed in His flames, and
through this He opens our eyes to see His goodness. He is Lord, and
He is worthy of reverence. He will never accept less.

Yes, Jesus has redeemed us and given us the ability to come before
His throne with boldness, but that does not mean we will be allowed to
do so irreverently. (See Hebrews 4:16.) The grace of God has been given
to us so we may approach Him. His grace should not reduce Him in
our eyes or bring Him down from the high place in our hearts. On the
contrary, it should increase our understanding and bring clarity to the
massive gulf between who we are and who God is. Who can ascend into
heaven? Who can call God down? To do so would be to make Him less,
which can never happen. We may be caught in deception about this, but
that does not change the greatness of our God or the truth of who He is.

To remind myself of my place before Him, I often kneel in God's
presence or even lie prostrate. I used to think my posture before God
wasn't a big deal, because I can humble my heart without physically
bending my knees. However, I have come to understand that it is my
pride that tells me that I don't need to humble myself before my King.
I don't always kneel or lie down, but I do know that if the thought of
kneeling comes to mind and I am not willing to do so, then I know that
I'm allowing pride to come between me and my Lord.

God of Grace

Did you know that "the kindness of God leads you to repentance"
(Romans 2:4)? And it is through the grace of God, because of His
love, that we receive this kindness. Grace can be defined as "unmerited

---

[6] A. W. Tozer, *The Knowledge of the Holy: The Attributes of God: Their Meaning in the Christian Life*, p. 27.

divine assistance given humans for their regeneration or sanctification."[7] Without God's amazing grace, we would have no hope of eternal life, salvation, redemption, or forgiveness of sins. We are utterly dependent on God's grace, which He lovingly gives to us as a gift.

It is God's wonderful grace that sets us back in right standing with Him, cleanses our stains of sin, and dresses us in a robe of righteousness. (See Isaiah 61:10.) His grace gives us abundant life and invites us to come close and know our Lord intimately. His grace is not, however, a free pass to do whatever we want. He will always extend His grace to us until the day of judgment, which He says will come like a thief in the night. (See 1 Thessalonians 5:2–7.) We do not want to be caught in rebellion or even complacency when He comes, so we should always be prepared for His return. We want to know in our hearts that we have served Him well.

Every day I want to love and serve my King, who loves me so much that He gave His grace to cover all the wretched parts of me. I want to serve my King, who brings me into life with Him. Does He not deserve this?

Grace can also be defined as "the power of God to enable Christians to live the new life in Christ."[8] In this sense, it is the grace of God that empowers us to live like Christ, be victorious, and change the world around us. God's grace is His power displayed in our lives. That's not the way we normally think about grace, but it's awesome!

The Glorious King

Lift up your heads, O gates,
And be lifted up, O ancient doors,
That the King of glory may come in!
Who is the King of glory?
The Lord strong and mighty,
The Lord mighty in battle.
Lift up your heads, O gates,

[7] *Merriam-Webster Dictionary.*
[8] *The International Standard Bible Encyclopedia*, vol. 2, p. 548.

And lift them up, O ancient doors,
That the King of glory may come in!
Who is this King of glory?
The Lord of hosts,
He is the King of glory.

—Psalm 24:7–10

We serve a king who is "high and lifted up" (Isaiah 6:1 KJV), a king who is said to shine like the sun. (See Revelation 1:16.) He has authority over everything on earth and in heaven. Satan is subject to Him, which is something I used to not think about much. (See Ephesians 1:20–22.) Every time I read in Isaiah about seeing the Lord on the throne, I wish I could have that same vision—to see God in His majesty as He truly is, and not just how I've imagined Him. Or to be like Moses and get a glimpse of His glory, even if it's His backside rather than His face.

The God we serve is greater and more glorious than anything we have to compare Him to on earth. But He gives us things like the sun as a small reminder of His powerful brilliance and intensity. He gives us the love of a husband and wife to give a little glimpse of His desire for a relationship with us. Everything we see here on earth is only a foreshadowing or a minuscule glimpse of who God is and what He has in store. The beauty of a sunset only echoes the beauty that is God. He is our glorious King who is worthy of adoration.

Lover of My Soul

Jesus, lover of my soul,
Let me to Thy bosom fly.

—Charles Wesley, "Jesus, Lover of My Soul"

Have you ever read the Song of Solomon? Some of the descriptions in this book are very intimate, such as when the author writes lovingly about his beloved's figure. I used to feel awkward when reading the Song of Solomon, partly because parts of it are so intimate. I didn't understand why this book is included in the Bible, but my understanding has since changed.

The Song of Solomon is not just a random book of the Bible. It is an important part of the Bible, God's personal letter to us. Song of Solomon is an allegorical story about how God feels about His bride. We are His bride, and He loves our form and longs for our attention. God wants to spend every minute of every day with us—sometimes praying and at other times in silence, sometimes serving and at other times working. He wants to be with us and love us through every part of our lives.

Does that mean it will always be easy and that we will always feel His closeness? No, sometimes we won't feel Him at all, but that does not mean He is not near. "He will be with you. He will not fail you or forsake you. Do not fear or be dismayed" (Deuteronomy 31:6). When we do not feel God's closeness, this is when the faith He gives us comes in. I know it can be hard, but standing in this faith is crucial.

Even though we will have moments of feeling far away from God's arms, there will also be times of glorious closeness with Him. He wants to draw us ever closer, until we breathe when He breathes and move when He moves. One day we will be that close to God, if that is the desire of our hearts. It might not happen on this earth, but it will be this way in heaven. God would not have sacrificed Himself for us if He did not deeply love us—who we are right now and who we will be one day. He saw us, loved us, and died for us. "While we were yet sinners, Christ died for us" (Romans 5:8).

God does not love us the way a brother loves a sister or a son loves a mother. God loves us as a husband loves his wife. It has always been a challenge for me to think of God as my husband. I'd think, *Isn't that sacrilegious or downright inappropriate?* It seemed strange to have romantic feelings for my Lord and Savior, but I've been working through this. Many scriptures point to this husband-and-wife kind of relationship between Christ and His church. (See Revelation 19, 20; Song of Solomon; Ephesians 5:25–33.)

Some people accept this intimate relationship as portrayed in scripture, but others find it much more difficult to believe. And even some who do believe in this intimate relationship with Jesus think that they will have to wait for heaven to actually experience it. But does our relationship with Jesus not start here? Are we not to grow in the knowledge of Christ daily? Paul says in Philippians 3:14 that even though he has not obtained it, he presses "on toward the goal for the prize." The prize is Christ, and our knowledge of Him and identification with Him will bring us so close in relationship to Him that we are changed into His glory.

We should not wait to press on toward Christ. Even though we can't fully understand it, that is not a sufficiently sound reason to put off growing and learning who He is in a deeper way. His Spirit is available to us right here and now, inviting us to draw near and learn how to become one with Him. Yes, we might have to wait for heaven to completely experience it or even to fully comprehend this relationship, but that doesn't mean we wait for heaven to start developing it. Our challenge is to experience a small part of who God is. Our joy is to press in and learn to become one with the lover of our souls. It starts now, this very minute. Why wait on heaven when He is here now and His Spirit is beckoning us to come close?

As a single woman, I have often looked at the idea of a relationship with God as applying only to the spiritual side of my life. Yes, He might help with my physical needs by providing things such as food, shelter, a job, and relationships, but I never thought of Him actually being the ultimate fulfillment of the relationship for which I longed. Yes, He is the lover of my soul, but what about my physical life?

For many years, I lived a life committed to God in word but not in action. I had become lost, giving way to the numbing effect of the world around me. Every once in a while I sensed Jesus calling me back to Him, but I put Him off for years. I was afraid to follow His calling, partly because of the scriptures about suffering for His name and glory. Also I hadn't experienced anything that felt like a real relationship between God and myself for many years, and I was afraid to commit wholeheartedly to someone I wasn't sure I trusted or even knew anymore.

And then, a couple of years ago, God made it very evident to me that it was time. So I took a step of faith and began giving Him every part of me: the scary and dirty parts, the distracted and numb parts, the broken parts, the anger and bitterness, the selfishness, the pride, the fear of being unloved, the fear of dying to myself, the rebellion against authority, the judgmental mindset, the laziness, the fear of being persecuted for Christ, the habits and impure daydreams.

God is still teaching me and working in me, removing my damaged parts and showing me how He can fill me instead with His love and righteousness. These last couple of years have not been completely easy, but I have never before felt this close to my Lover. All I want is more. There is no end to Him, and I want to dive deeper and deeper still. He has redeemed me because of His love for me. I would not trade this relationship for anything—not for a husband, kids, an easy life, or all the money in the world. I can imagine no earthly experience that could ever possibly compare to my Beloved.

God desires this kind of close relationship and more with everyone. If we come to Him with abandon, He will meet us in a better way than we possibly could have imagined. But we can't hold anything back. Our Lover will be satisfied only with every part of us.

5

LIVING FOR WHAT?

You are the only one in my head
I've chosen you now my heart is set
Your voice forever it is my strength, my strength ...
When You speak, dreams and reality collide
Your word rewrites my destiny
My life finds a new beginning
'Cause You are, You are my energy.
—Hillsong Young & Free, "Energy"

From a young age, many of us wonder what we will be when we grow up. As we make our way through high school, we wonder what we should do with our lives. When we graduate from college and launch our careers, we might pray about it, hoping to get direction from God. As the years pass, many of us continue to wonder why we are here. Is there something specific that we should be spending our lives doing?

Many Christians have a deep sense that they are supposed to do something important with their lives. As time goes on, however, we tend to stuff this feeling farther down and try to ignore it, because it confuses us and leaves us feeling lost. And who enjoys feeling lost? So we can keep trying to silence this nagging feeling by filling our lives with anything that comforts and/or distracts us, or we can try to find the purpose of our lives in things such as relationships and vocations.

Let's talk about this deep desire, its importance, and what happens when we don't listen to it.

Does Everyone Live for the Same Thing?

No, we don't. However, we all *should* be living for the same thing, with every breath we take. This might seem like a very generic thing to say, but when we break this down, it actually begins to look very individualized. When I say we should be all living for the same thing, I mean that with every breath, thought, action, dream, and hope, we should bring glory to ourselves …

No, wait! We should bring glory *only* to Jesus Christ, the King of all creation, who died a tortured and bloody death for you and me. The problem is that our prideful old way of thinking doesn't actually want us to live this way, and yet the matter of choosing for whom we will live will ultimately be the crux of our lives. This is the most important decision we will ever make, and yet it is complicated by the fact that we are forced to make it over and over again, every day. Even though we have decided, once and forever, to give our lives and hearts to God, we are still faced with the need to choose God in our actions every day.

Do We Have To?

God's gift of salvation is free, but it has one string attached: we must believe in Jesus. "Therefore I said to you that you will die in your sins; for unless you believe that I am He, you will die in your sins" (John 8:24). To truly believe means to repent and change our ways. The proof of our believing in Him should be evident by the change in our daily lives. Our works, the expression of our lives, should give evidence of our faith. (See James 2:17–18.) Jesus says, "He who believes in the Son has eternal life; but he who does not obey the Son will not see life, but the wrath of God abides on him" (John 3:36).

Obedience is required of us, whether we feel like doing it or not. In the Ten Commandments, God says for children to obey their parents so that they will live long in the place God gives them. (See Exodus

20:12.) And in Ephesians 6:2–3, Paul says, "Honor your father and mother (which is the first commandment with a promise), so that it may be well with you, and that you may live long on the earth." Paul's words also refer to our relationship with God. Just as children are to obey their parents here on earth, so we are to obey God, our heavenly Father. By honoring our parents, we will enjoy long life on earth, and by honoring God as our Father, we obtain the gift of eternal life. God is a good Father.

True belief means changing our ways and obeying Him. One of the main ways we obey God is by living our lives for Him, rather than for ourselves. One of the ways Jesus calls us to obey is to daily die to ourselves. Jesus mentions over and over in the Gospels the need for us to come to Him and die. (See Matthew 10:38, 16:25–26; Luke 9:23, 14:26; Mark 8:35, 10:29–30; John 12:24–25.) "Whoever does not carry his own cross and come after Me cannot be my disciple" (Luke 14:27).

This is a hard scriptural topic that we often avoid, but it is so very important. Just as Jesus lived in obedience to God, we also are to live in obedience to God. (See Hebrews 5:8–9.) If we die to self, we can be raised to life in Jesus. This is not a one-time choice, but a daily one. When we choose His ways over ours, we are living in His resurrection life. This doesn't mean that we can earn our salvation, but in a very real way, our obedience is proof of our salvation.

The consequence of refusing to submit to God and live for Him is the same as what would have happened to Esther if she had refused to intercede for herself and her people. "For if you remain silent at this time, relief and deliverance will arise for the Jews from another place and you and your father's house will perish" (Esther 4:14). God will always have His way. All we do is decide whether to help Him or end up being destroyed by Him. Destruction may come now or later, but it will come for those who are not faithful. That is not His will for us, for He desires us to "abound with blessings" (Proverbs 28:20), but we must be faithful and not live for our own gain.

To help guide us in understanding God and His will for us, He has woven themes throughout scripture from beginning to end. He is God, Lord of creation, who is worthy of praise, and He loves us so much, He does not hold anything good back from us. (See Genesis 1:1, Revelation 4:11, James 1:17.) "For the Lord God is a sun and shield; The Lord gives grace and glory; No good thing does He withhold from those *who walk uprightly*" (Psalm 84:11; emphasis added).

God knew before the creation of the world that Adam and Eve would sin in the garden. He knew we would be alive today. He knew before He created the world that He would have to send His Son to die on a cross for Adam, Eve, you, me, and everyone else. And yet He still created the world because He wanted to spend eternity with us. He loves us that much! Even knowing the cost beforehand, He still chose us with joy.

This God who loves us infinitely has told us to "Sin no more" (John 8:11). God is holy and will not suffer to dwell with anyone who is sinful. God has said that we are to be holy and that all our behavior should be holy. This sounds daunting, and obviously we could never attain the holiness required of God on our own, but Christ has given us this holiness. God knows us and our weaknesses, but He also knows the power of His Son and His Spirit who lives in us.

Just as God the Father, Jesus, and the Holy Spirit are one, He also desires to be one with us. Holiness from us is required to obtain this oneness with God. Since we can't do this on our own, Christ has given His life, so that we can have His holiness. And through His holiness we can dwell with God. But this requires us to want the holiness of God, which in turn requires us to live our lives not for ourselves but for Him, and to live in a holy way.

This Looks Like What?

Only by complete surrender can we even hope to comprehend a glimmer of God's holiness and therefore live this holiness. Only by living at the foot of the cross and daily dying to self can we begin to understand the truth of who God is. The only reason we can stand before the King of glory is that when we kneel in surrender at His feet, He has the joy of lifting us to our feet before Him.

We must be willing to put God first, to step down from the thrones of our lives and allow God to reign there, and to forsake our own dreams and desires in support of His. We might say, "But God gave me these dreams," or perhaps, "Can't God's dreams for me be the same dreams I already have?" He does give us dreams, and His dreams and ours can be the same. Nonetheless, He wants us to know that He is Lord of our hearts and that nothing should be more important to us than Him. He wants us to come to Him and dwell with Him—not for answers to prayers, but for God Himself. He wants us to love to be with Him, trust Him, and seek out His heart.

Too many of us don't passionately and honestly seek God for Himself. Are we trying to learn to trust Him in all things? God's heart is constantly crying out for us. He wants us to desire to draw close to Him and look on the face of our King, rather than focus on what He could give us.

This requires a heart change—nothing less will do. This heart change starts where all new life begins, with the power of Christ and the awakening of the Holy Spirit, but that is only the beginning of new life. Any form of new life needs food to grow. We don't look at a new seedling and think, *It doesn't need water, sun, good soil, and conducive temperatures to grow.* No, we know that if we don't provide these things, the plant will die.

Why do we think that our new lives with Christ are any different? Are we not supposed to find ways to help ourselves grow in the Lord? Should we not read His Word daily, to water our hearts and minds? Should we not choose to run after God and learn more about who He is? When we choose to seek Him wholeheartedly, our desire for Him only increases. And if we don't know how to choose God daily, then we should ask Him to show us. We need His wisdom in all things, including this. "If any of you lacks wisdom, let him ask of God, who gives to all generously and without reproach, and it will be given to him. But he must ask in faith without any doubting" (James 1:5–6).

When we decide to seek the Lord with all our hearts, and we feel a desire to learn how to put Him first, then we are starting to live in the "fear of the Lord," which means living in reverence toward God. "The fear of the Lord is the beginning of wisdom, and the knowledge of the Holy One is understanding" (Proverbs 9:10). So we are already on the right track!

Stewardship

Stewardship is one of the most important concepts for us to understand when talking about living for God. Jesus told a few parables about the importance of stewardship. (See Matthew 25 and Luke 16.) With God's help, we must remember that everything we have is borrowed. Our time, resources, relationships—every breath we take—is entrusted to us by God.

It is our joy and pleasure in life to learn how to be good stewards by putting God's possessions to their best use. This process can take time, but gradually, by God's grace, it will become second nature. We can practice good stewardship with everything, from the gas we put in the car to the extra bottle of nail polish we buy, from cleaning our houses to how we care for our families, from the time we spend watching TV to the thoughts we ponder, from the mission groups we support to our regular tithe.

One day we will be held accountable for *everything* we do in life: "For we must all appear before the judgment seat of Christ, so that each one may be recompensed for his deeds in the body, according to what he has done, whether good or bad" (2 Corinthians 5:10).

I'm so thankful that we don't have to do this through our own strength. Only through God's grace are we able to steward anything well. As we spend time with Him and allow Him the space and time to work in, through, and for us, He will walk us faithfully through these challenges.

Areas of Stewardship

I want to spend a little time discussing a few of the areas in which God has been working a change in me. This is not a comprehensive list, but for me these have been major areas of stewardship focus.

Money

Stewardship includes how we use the money with which God blesses us, but most people don't think about—or don't *want* to think about—being a good steward of their money for God. Are we spending our money for our own benefit or for the benefit of God? All the money we have is really His.

It's hard for me to remember this when I'm shopping, because I spend a lot of time thinking about what I want for myself and my friends. But I'm learning to ask myself, every time I walk into a store, whether what I am about to buy is the best use of my money. Am I being a wise steward with my money?

There's nothing wrong with spending money on ourselves or other people, but it's always important to give the Lord a chance to weigh in on our use of His money. Often His desires for our money are different from what we might expect. For instance, after I had saved almost half the money I needed as a down payment on a house, I began sensing that God wanted me to use the money for something else. In fact, He wanted me to give it to some people who were in need, and so I prayerfully chose to obey Him. I knew He would take care of me, and He continues to do so every day. He is an amazing Father!

Thoughts

Our thought life is a major area where we need to understand the importance of our stewardship. When we daydream, how would we feel if we knew that Jesus could see what we are imagining and hear what we are thinking? Well, He already does. Unfortunately it took me years to really take this understanding to heart enough to change the way I was thinking. Psalm 139:2–4 says, "You understand my thought from afar. You scrutinize my path and my lying down, And are intimately acquainted with all my ways. Even before there is a word on my tongue, Behold, O Lord, You know it all."

If we let these verses sink in, we realize how intense they are. We all have thoughts that we keep to ourselves because ... Well, we just wouldn't want to be caught thinking them. However, we have already been caught—by our Lord and Savior. Christ doesn't condemn us for our thoughts, but we need to learn how to be careful with them and submit them to God. This is a discipline that takes time to turn into a consistent habit.

When Jesus talks in Matthew about how to live and the sins we commit, He actually raises the bar of accountability from our actions to our thoughts. He says that if we look at another person and lust after them, then we have already committed adultery in our hearts. (See Matthew 5:28.) He is not only warning us against lustful thoughts, but also trying to help us understand that we are accountable for all our thoughts. When we daydream about something we shouldn't or curse someone in our thoughts, that sin hurts the heart of God. Our thoughts have power because they affect our souls, and sinful thoughts can affect our souls for eternity. If our thoughts can be sinful, then they have weight that effects our souls and therefore our eternities. Wow! But there is hope in Christ, who is happy to help each of us come closer to His holiness. Only He has the ability to breathe this holiness into our lives, but we have to choose to follow Him, even in our thoughts.

Time

Another big issue for most people is how we spend our time. What's a normal day for us? How do we start our days, and what is our daily routine? Do we spend a lot of time on things of no value? Many of the things we find ourselves doing are a waste of time. Activities such as surfing the Internet, updating our online status, watching movies, and reading books can take a lot of our time. When we are done with them, what have we really gained? None of these things are bad in and of themselves, but we should avoid engaging in such activities excessively and make certain to choose edifying forms of them.

Activity that brings us closer to God can take many forms—being alone with Him, serving others, watching certain movies, reading certain books, spending time with friends, working at being a good employee, and even washing the dishes. So why are we spending our time on anything else? Some of us might answer, "Because it's fun" or "Because I need an escape."

I said those same things for years and years. Eventually I tired of wasting my time escaping, and I felt empty from not doing things with true worth. But I didn't know how to change, so I just kept doing empty things. Then God opened my eyes to the value of time, which passes as quickly as a wisp of smoke. I began to understand that God wants to be our only escape and the basis of our fun. He wants our relationship with Him to be so close that we do everything in and through Him.

It can be overwhelming to realize that nothing in life is worth doing if it is not done for Christ, but when we rest in Him, He helps us live in the freedom of His life. I'm starting to understand what it means to dwell in the presence of God and use our time and resources for Him. He cleans the clutter and brokenness out of our lives, and replaces them with hope and joy.

We have to be willing to give it all up for Him. If we are not willing to put everything—our money, time, resources, energy, and thoughts—on the altar for the glory of the Lord of the universe, then we have not actually committed ourselves fully to Him. To the extent that we have fully surrendered ourselves to God, our hearts will be open and malleable, enabling us to receive and use His gifts properly. God and His Spirit are the ultimate gifts. He is not a sad substitute for earthly things. He is the best we could ever hope for, and far more than we can handle. I dare you to try.

Caution

In this section, I would like to offer cautionary remarks about a few of our culture's prevalent mentalities.

Blessings

We are under constant pressure to buy into the world's standards for what should and shouldn't be. Such standards can become so ingrained in us, whether or not we realize it, that they become the gauge by which we measure the extent to which we are blessed and living a good life. But is this really a biblical idea?

This worldview of a good life is taught in many churches today. The message is that if we follow God, His blessings will fall on us from heaven. The Bible does say this in some places, but it doesn't usually say what form the blessing will take. (See Proverbs 10:22, Malachi 3:10.) We might have a preconceived idea about exactly how God is going to bless us, especially if we compare what we have with the things that people around us have, but we will often be wrong. There are many scriptures about God providing our needs, but most scripture that mentions the ways in which we are blessed points us back to our relationship with God. (See Philippians 4:19.)

"Blessed is the one who trusts in the Lord, whose confidence is in him. They will be like a tree planted by the water that sends out its roots by the stream. It does not fear when heat comes; its leaves are always green. It has no worries in a year of drought and never fails to bear fruit" (Jeremiah 17:7–8 NIV). Our foundation, our one true blessing, is God. Yes, He provides our needs, but the blessing is God Himself, not what He gives to us. Jeremiah is showing the goodness of God by describing His blessings. The provisions are meant only to point us back to our Provider.

"The Lord bless you and keep you; the Lord make his face shine on you and be gracious to you; the Lord turn his face toward you and give you peace" (Numbers 6:24–26 NIV).

"The Lord is my shepherd, I lack nothing. He makes me lie down in green pastures, he leads me beside quiet waters, he refreshes my soul. He guides me along the right paths for his name's sake" (Psalm 23:1–2 NIV).

"Taste and see that the Lord is good; blessed is the one who takes refuge in him" (Psalm 34:8 NIV).

These verses speak of how the presence of the Lord blesses and therefore changes our lives. God and His presence are the most important blessings we can ever received, and they will change our physical and spiritual lives in ways we can't even fathom.

Entitlement

Another mind-set of which we should be cautious is thinking that if we snap our fingers at God, He will give us what we desire. He is *God*. He does not have to give us anything at all, yet because He is good, He loves to give good gifts to His children. (See Matthew 7:11, James 1:17.) This reminds me of what C. S. Lewis says in *The Weight of Glory*: "For He claims all, because He is love and must bless. He cannot bless us unless He has us. When we try to keep within us an area that is our own, we try to keep an area of death. Therefore, in love, He claims all. There's no bargaining with Him."[9]

---

[9] C. S. Lewis, *The Weight of Glory*, p. 190.

God does promise that He will give us the desires of our hearts. But most people don't read the entire verse, which says, "Delight yourself in the Lord; and He will give you the desires of your heart" (Psalm 37:4). For us to delight in someone, we must really treasure that person. We must desire the best for them and want to become intimate with them. When we have become intimate with someone, his or her desires tend to rub off on us.

If we become intimate with Jesus, eventually His desires and ours will be the same. If we are close with another person, would we choose to do something that would grieve him or her? Would we knowingly do something to which our intimate friend is completely opposed? No, of course not. Similarly, we shouldn't want to do anything that would sadden the heart of God, our most intimate friend.

This learning process takes an entire lifetime, and we have to work on it every day. We haven't signed up for an easy road—this is a hard road. In some ways the road is straight and narrow, and yet to a trained eye our road is wide and beautiful when we learn to understand how to walk in the freedom God gives. Few people actually submit to this path which at first looks so hard, so they never get any closer to Jesus and therefore don't see it's beauty.

Distractions

Anything but God is a distraction. Even our families, relationships, and service to others can distract us from God. They can pull us away from thinking about loving Him, and point us toward our selfish desires, regardless of whether those desires are about ourselves or others whom we love.

Did not Jesus say, "If anyone comes to Me, and does not hate his own father and mother and wife and children and brothers and sisters, yes and even his own life, he cannot be My disciple" (Luke 14:26)? This is a hard scripture for most people to accept, but God doesn't mean that we should actually hate anyone. Clearly other scriptures tell us to

Ruth Wilcox

not hate. (See Leviticus 19:17, 1 John 2:8–11, 1 John 3:14–15.) But in Luke, Jesus is showing us how strongly we should be committed to our relationship with Him. He is using such strong language to get through to us. Above all else, we should think of Him, love Him, and plan our lives around Him.

This would be a hard challenge no matter what culture we lived in, but in our Western culture, which is all about what we want, this is huge. This is why what Paul says in Romans 12:2 is so important: "And do not be conformed to this world, but be transformed by the renewing of your mind, so that you may prove what the will of God is, that which is good and acceptable and perfect." Whatever we are constantly looking at, thinking about, and seeking—that's what we are being conformed to. We can choose to be conformed to God's ways and words by reading about Him, spending time with Him, and talking about Him. We will be transformed by renewing our minds in Him, worshipping Him, praying, and focusing on His Word. When we allow Him to transform us, then we will know how to live for Him, what He desires, and what is truly good.

Living for Christ

Sometimes we will have to "suffer according to the will of God" (1 Peter 4:19). Did not Paul suffer? Did not the apostles suffer for Christ and His message of hope? We have sisters and brothers in Christ who are suffering for His name all over the world today. In Asia, the Middle East, and Africa, for example, people are being killed, maimed, and starved to death for the witness they are bringing to the world for Christ.

Meanwhile, what are we doing? Sitting in our comfortable homes, driving our nice cars, going out with friends for dinner, and so on. And yet we complain if our computers crash, our air conditioners break down, or our food doesn't turn out just right. God wants good things for us, so we should enjoy the things we are given and praise Him for

74

them. But are these things really our biggest worries? Are our eyes focused only on ourselves? It is easy to be distracted by our easy and free culture, but we should be using our freedom here to serve God openly. "From everyone who has been given much, much will be required; and to whom they entrusted much, of him they will ask all the more" (Luke 12:48).

Where are our lives showing the work of God, and how are we using the things He has entrusted to us? Living for Christ should mean going against the grain of our culture and the world. If Christ truly were our reason for living, even our friends would probably tease us for being different. We would encounter strong opposition from the world around us. We would not fit in at most places, including some churches. We need to be the light of Christ everywhere we go and in everything we do, no matter how hard it is.

Even though this doesn't sound easy or comfortable, this is the life we have told God we will accept, in return for His forgiveness, life, and love. When we say we are Christians, we need to choose God's path. If we don't, we are living fake Christian lives, claiming with our words to be His, but denying Christ with our actions. If we deny knowing Him here, He will deny knowing us when we stand before God. (See Matthew 10:33.)

Few Christians believe that they are denying Christ in their lives. After all, when someone asks if we're Christians, we answer affirmatively. But denying Christ actually means denying to *choose* Christ, which runs much deeper. Do we choose Him when deciding what topic to discuss with our friends or what words to use in conversation? Do we choose Him when deciding what movie to watch or what music to listen to? Do we choose Him when we spend our time daydreaming? If we aren't choosing Him with our every decision, then we are choosing to deny Him. This is how deeply we affect God's heart with everything we do. The choices we make daily bring Him either joy or sorrow, and it is important for us to understand this.

This is something with which I'll probably struggle for the rest of my life. I don't like creating waves in my life, but as I grow to love Him more and more, I also have a growing desire for holiness in my life and the things with which I surround myself. I can no longer tolerate degrading conversations, TV shows, or books. I don't want to spend money wastefully or look at sexual things. With every choice for holiness, I am learning to choose Him over this world. I want to proclaim Him and His holiness to those around me with the testimony of my life, not in a judgmental way, but with grace and love by the leading of the Holy Spirit.

How It Will Affect Your World

Surrounded by darkness, we are to be the "light of the world" (Matthew 5:14). For many of us, even our own lives exist in darkness, but that is our choice. If we have denied the call of Christ to live as His light, we should take a hard look at our lives to see the truth of what we're doing. Where have we seen God moving in our lives? Are we seeking His heart? Do we desire to be close to Him even in small choices? What do we do with our time? Do we choose to spend time with Him, even when we might want to do other things? Where does He rank in importance for us?

God says, "Seek first His Kingdom and His righteousness, and all these things will be added to you" (Matthew 6:33). He's talking about our daily needs and how we shouldn't worry about what to eat, where to live, or what to wear. As He takes care of the beast of the world, will He not also take care of us? It's important to remember, however, that we must seek God and His righteousness *first*—not when we feel like it or when it's easy. When God is first, nothing else will have the same weight. Everything will have more clarity through Him. He will provide all our needs, and He knows what is necessary for us to live for Him.

Living for Christ alone will change the dynamics of our lives forever. We will see everything—*everything*—differently. Things we didn't previously care about or even notice, such as a neighbor who needs help moving something, will suddenly become opportunities to show our love for Christ. Everything we do, we should do for Christ.

Loving Christ has taught me how to love other people. As an ER nurse, I see people in bad situations daily, including people who do not want help or just want us to help them continue their bad habits. We patch them up and send them back to their bad life situations. These people usually are very demanding and get upset when we can't or won't give them whatever they want. They don't seem to be able to to improve their lives, so they come back again and again with the same issues. Even when their situations get worse, they choose to continue their bad habits.

I used to get annoyed by the bad life choices made by such people, instead of seeing an opportunity to pray that they would come to know Jesus and His freedom. But now when a person like that comes in, I ask God to let me love him or her like I love Him. That doesn't mean giving that person whatever he or she wants. For our own good, God doesn't give any of us whatever we want. But He wants us to love *everyone* and treat each person with respect and care. My natural tendency is to show little mercy to people whom I think should have learned their lesson by now. Yet God says we are to forgive seventy times seven, which really means as many times as it takes.

To forgive, we must show mercy. James 2:13 says, "For judgment will be merciless to one who has shown no mercy; mercy triumphs over judgment." God also tells us to "love mercy" (Micah 6:8 NIV). This means that we shouldn't show mercy begrudgingly, but instead learn to love mercy so much that we will love to show it to others. God is telling us to be merciful to others, whether it is easy or not. God does not tell us to do things that we would naturally do, because what would be the point? But He is constantly telling us to do things that we can do only through the power of Christ.

One way to demonstrate the love of Christ is to show mercy to people who need it. Living this way will change our world, if we allow merciful love to shine through our daily lives to those around us. Sure, we can safely hide from the harsh world as it rages around us with its desires and lusts—but hiding is really just denying God. Or we can devote ourselves to God, sit at His feet, and become so close with Him that we will know what He desires and then go and do it. This is what it means to live in the power of Christ, who has made us right with God. Christ is the only way anyone may draw close to God.

Do you want God to use you? Or are you going to hide in your personal cave of selfish desires and distractions, and therefore miss out on a close relationship with God? If you hide, you will forfeit a life-changing relationship that would allow God to work through you. Having Christ as the focus of your life will not only change how you see the simple daily tasks given to you, but also show you how to love the world around you when you are walking in His steps. Christ can turn you into a light on a hill that draws people to Him.

6

TRUE FULFILLMENT

I want to be the only one on the throne of your heart.
The only one that moves you.

I will remove the names of your lovers,
Even the memory of their face fades away.
I will write on you my name forever.
I will be known by you as faithful and true ...

So come back, come back,
I'll take you to your first love.

—Harvest, "Only One"

Who can claim to know what true fulfillment is? Who has experienced its glory? It's awesome to know that through God's love, we are doing—in the right time and place—what we are meant to do. Most of us feel joy occasionally when things seem right, and we have a sense of the inner peace that accompanies this joy. It is at these times that we gain a glimpse of true fulfillment.

What Is True Fulfillment?

I used to think that things such as my friends, family, car, and home helped fulfill me. They never truly satisfied me, however, although I count them as rich blessings. Instead, they have served as signposts to point me toward my true source of fulfillment.

For many years, I experienced a deep, quiet need to let God fulfill me, but I suppressed that persistent whisper and instead tried to fill my life with what I saw around me. The problem was that it never worked. I learned over the years how to find things that made me feel better, but that wasn't a perfect fix. I knew that I probably needed to go back to God to find the answer, but I didn't want to give Him my all, and I knew that was exactly what He wanted.

Finally God gave me an ultimatum—either Him or me. He said, "You are getting lost in the world. One more misstep and you are going to miss out on the plans I have for your life. If you don't choose Me now, there will be no going back to recover what I have planned for you." It was as if someone grabbed me by the shoulders, stared me in the eyes, and pleaded with me. I knew then that I wanted whatever life He had planned for me. The sense of urgency was overwhelming, so by His grace, I chose Him.

I have since come to see that true fulfillment does not mean having everything the world can offer. Nor does it necessarily mean doing the things I had originally desired in life. Only through serving and living for Christ can we gain the pure joy of true fulfillment.

When Paul was following Christ's example by living on the go, preaching His Word, and being tortured for the promise of Christ's sacrifice, he felt this fulfillment. Does this mean he never had questions or always knew where and when he should be taking his ministry? No. According to his letters, he sometimes wished to be with those to whom he was writing, but he didn't know when that would happen. At times he was prevented from visiting his brothers and sisters in Christ, because he had to continue his ministry elsewhere. Paul's goal was not self-fulfillment, but Christ fulfillment. He sometimes wanted other things, but he always came back to doing the will of Jesus, which is God's will. He did not consider his sufferings as anything compared with the glory to come. (See Romans 8:18.) All he cared about was allowing the Holy Spirit to speak through him and living his life the way God wanted him to. Paul's life ended in martyrdom, but he served God with joy even unto death.

While He was here on earth, Jesus did not live for Himself but for His Father. He did only what He saw His Father doing in heaven, and yet He lived a fulfilling life. (See John 5:19.)

Despite our suffering, joy comes in the morning. Christ is worth anything we might go through, and He will be with us and give us His joy through it all. His joy might not always be overwhelming, but it will always bring us peace.

As I learn to live my life in and through Christ, I find that joy and true fulfillment are closely linked. Where one is, the other is sure to abound. I'm also realizing the distinction between happiness and joy. Being happy in a worldly sense isn't the same as experiencing true joy. There should be more to life than feeling happy, which is a fleeting emotion based on our relationships with other people or the possessions we gain.

"Do not store up for yourselves treasures on earth, where moth and rust destroy, and where thieves break in and steal" (Matthew 6:19). Earthly treasures such as money, clothes, cars, gadgets, makeup, shoes, and purses—and certainly relationships with other people—can be a source of happiness, but they should not be the main focus of our hearts. "For where your treasure is, there your heart will be also" (Matthew 6:21).

We should treasure the important people in our lives, but we should also be careful that Jesus is our ultimate treasure. No person or thing should take His place in our hearts. When He is the King of our hearts, we can begin to understand the joy that He gives us in mind, body, and spirit. The joy of the Lord is something that works from the inside out. It comes from the Lord, who dwells in us, and not from our circumstances. Worldly happiness works in the opposite direction, from the outside in. A change in our worldly circumstances can make us happy, but that's not an emotion that endures.

Are we okay with the world's happiness, which often results from closing our eyes to the true value of our lives, or are we going to accept the reality of Jesus and begin living for Him? He is the only One who can give complete fulfillment and lasting joy, which will become the constant undertone of our lives. Even in our daily challenges, we can look to Jesus and find joy in His presence. He is always with us, and His joy is always available.

True fulfillment is a blessing from God. It is not something we can gain from this world, no matter how hard we try. It's easy to get distracted and try to satisfy this desire for fulfillment with whatever is available. We can work our way up the career ladder—get a bigger salary, a better office, and lots of perks—but that will never truly satisfy us. We could have a very large family with lots of children, the perfect husband, and a beautiful home, but that will never fulfill our deep inner desire. We could travel all over the world and add lots of customs stamps to our passports, which might distract us for a while, but it will inevitably leave us with the same lack of fulfillment.

We'll always want more, because we are an insatiable people. That's why it is so crucial to find the true source of lasting fulfillment—and to find it *now* and stop wasting our brief lives. As A. W. Tozer says in *The Knowledge of the Holy*, "Because we are the handiwork of God, it follows that all our problems and their solutions are theological."[10] We all have a deep desire for *something* in life. Many people don't recognize this desire as a longing for God, but they know that something is missing. C. S. Lewis writes about this in *Mere Christianity*:

> If I find in myself a desire which no experience in this world
> can satisfy, the most probable explanation is that I was made
> for another world. If none of my earthly pleasures satisfy it,
> that does not prove that the universe is a fraud. Probably
> earthly pleasures were never meant to satisfy it, but only to

---

[10] A. W. Tozer, *The Knowledge of the Holy: The Attributes of God: Their Meaning in the Christian Life*, p. 27.

arouse it, to suggest the real thing. If that is so, I must take care, on the one hand, never to despise, or be unthankful for, these earthly blessings, and on the other, never to mistake them for the something else of which they are only a kind of copy, or echo, or mirage. I must keep alive in myself the desire for my true country, which I shall not find till after death; I must never let if get snowed under or turned aside; I must make it the main object of life to press on to that other country and to help others to do the same.[11]

It is only when we choose to fill this desire with God that we will start to glimpse satisfaction. We will constantly want more of Him because His presence is so good. As A. W. Tozer says simply in *The Pursuit of God*, "O God, I have tasted Thy goodness, and it has both satisfied me and made me thirsty for more."[12]

Things of this world were originally meant to show God's love for us and give us opportunities to show God our love for Him. But after the fall of man, sin entered the world and immediately began changing things meant for beauty into things that now possess only a small measure of God's original beauty. Now, instead of pointing to God and His goodness, earthly things point to us, our selfish desires, and our pride. Everything in life has been warped toward our own self-satisfaction, and thus we are easily distracted from the glorious God of life. We desperately need to be brought back to the beginning, where our hearts were created to commune with Him in love. If only we would seek God and His heart *first* in our lives, then we would gain true understanding of what it means to be fulfilled.

---

[11] C. S. Lewis, *Mere Christianity*, p. 136–137.

[12] A. W. Tozer, *The Pursuit of God*, p. 6.

What We Can Do

God says in His Word that we are to work out our salvation with fear and trembling. (See Philippians 2:12.) When we come to the Creator of the world to repent and receive redemption, we should do this in reverence. This is the most important thing we will ever do for ourselves—accepting Jesus Christ's sacrifice and asking Him to cleanse our souls and make them whole. Until this step has been taken, we will never find true fulfillment in our lives, no matter how hard we try.

Beyond this, we must work out how our lives should be lived. Our salvation is a complete change from death to life, and the changes in our hearts will be discovered only through a lifelong process. As a good friend of mine said, "We can look back to the moment when we were saved, just as a bride can look back at the moment she was wed to her lover, but similarly to a marriage, salvation does not end after the ceremony. The wedding lasts an hour, but the marriage will continue for years afterward." This is how we should view our lives in relation to our salvation.

We are to carry our crosses and die every day. Understanding this will come in stages, which is part of the process of working out our salvation. We can't just do it once and then push it into the corner of our lives, but we are to allow our salvation to have a continuous effect on our lives. We are to daily learn what it means to be saved and redeemed, and learn how our salvation has made us dead to the world but alive to Christ. This process will require time and a lot of effort, but we have to start here. Jesus is the only way to the Father. (See John 14:6.) Accepting His salvation, and then actually living a life with Christ, is the only way to go forward.

When we have begun working out our salvation, God will help us begin to understand our desires. Sometimes He gives us a desire that makes sense and can be fulfilled in a normal way, but at other times He gives us desires that will not be fulfilled in ways we can understand, at least not at first. It would be naïve and even prideful to think that we will learn to always understand the ways of God, whose thoughts are much greater than we could ever fathom. But the closer to Him we get, the clearer He will make the things in life that are important to us. The more clearly we see the face of God, the more we start to truly understand who we are and the purpose of our lives. By understanding these things, we can start to comprehend how true fulfillment can be found.

Companionship

One of my deepest longings in life has been for true, faithful companionship. I always had my eyes open for people who would satisfy this desire in me, but the few people I found here and there, even though I loved to be with them, never completely satisfied me. I had my small group of girlfriends who helped to partially satisfy my desire for companionship, but there was still something lacking. It didn't matter what I did or with whom I tried to be friends, I always longed for something more. I was a Christian, but I was not seeking God with hunger and thirst. I was instead seeking relationships with people and experiences around me, thinking they were what I needed. Unsatisfied, I started to think I would never find "the one my heart loves" (Song of Solomon 3:4 NIV). I kept living as if I was made for earthly relationships more than I was made for a relationship with Christ.

The true purpose of my desire for companionship is and will always be to point me to God, and its ultimate fulfillment will be in the Lord. As a flesh-and-bone human being, I feel a definite need for another person to satisfy this longing, and yet I realized that anyone who stepped into that role would end up failing me, without understanding why or how. The only one who can successfully assume this role in my life is God. Marriage is a gift from God, designed to show us a small glimpse of how our relationship with God should be. It can actually muffle the acuteness of our desire for God for years, but eventually we realize that our deep desire for companionship still isn't satisfied. Then we end up feeling depressed and lost, wondering whether the problem is physical or psychological. Tragically, some people choose to accept their loneliness and live out their lives that way.

Unfortunately, many women are so afraid of being alone that they will put up with abuse just to have someone there at least part of the time. In contrast, God will be there always, but people often don't think that holds the same weight as having a human companion. What is a human companion compared with almighty God? He can far outstrip anyone in His ability to provide comfort and companionship, but only if we seek Him first. Just as any good relationship takes time and effort, unless we seek Jesus with all our heart, we will never completely grasp understanding in this area.

Some people become frustrated after thinking they have been wholeheartedly seeking the Lord. If we get frustrated to the point of being angry with God, then we have not really given Him everything, and He is not really everything to us, or we really aren't listening to what He is telling us. God longs to be all that we desire, but it takes time to develop this in our hearts. He plants the seed through the Holy Spirit, but we have to take time and put in the effort to allow this seed to be cultivated. Once we have grown in loving Him, He will trust us with His heart. To be honored with the knowledge of God's heart—who can fathom that?

As daughters of the King, why do we allow ourselves to enter into relationships with companions who do not cherish us? God has such a heart to see us bloom and grow into the amazing women He created us to be, but these relationships in which we sometimes get entangled are poisonous water to the flowers of our lives. Why are we willing to pay this high price for destructive companionship? Because we have not learned the true, loving nature of God. If we did truly see His nature, then not only would we gain true satisfaction, but we would actually long for Him more deeply than for anyone else.

After walking this road of loneliness for many years, I have started to comprehend this truth. Over the last few years, as I have sought after God alone and allowed Him to purify me and purge me of things in my life, I have learned more about His love. I am finally in the place of wanting Him above any other relationship. The completeness of His companionship is more fulfilling than anything else I have ever experienced.

Even though it is His desire for many of us to have husbands, God does not want this person to come anywhere close to having the importance He holds in our lives. In the scriptures, Paul writes to single women about how becoming married changes the way we live, and about how free we are, as single women, to live for God alone. Just as anything we experience right now on this earth, marriage can be not only a blessing but also a challenge to our relationships with God. First Corinthians 7:34–35 says, "The woman who is unmarried, and the virgin, is concerned about the things of the Lord, that she may be holy both in body and spirit; but one who is married is concerned about the things of the world, how she may please her husband. This I say for your own benefit; not to put a restraint upon you, but to promote what is appropriate and to secure undistracted devotion to the Lord."

Please hear me when I say this. Not being a virgin doesn't mean that we are somehow disqualified and that Paul's message doesn't apply to us. Through Christ there is forgiveness for anything we have done, and He redeems us. To *redeem* means to "gain or regain possession of (something) in exchange for payment."[13] Praise God, Jesus has already made the payment on the cross for our redemption! He no longer sees our past sins, but only His own righteousness and holiness covering us. He loves us, and when we choose Him, He will give us "a crown of beauty for ashes" (Isaiah 61:3 NLT).

For years, every time I read 1 Corinthians 7:34–35, I thought, *Paul you're crazy. How can you say this?* I would always counter that passage with Ephesians 5:28–29, which describes how the relationship of a

---

[13] *English Oxford Living Dictionaries.*

husband and wife is supposed to point to Christ's love for the church. And I would say to God that in order for me to truly understand the love of Christ, I needed to be married. That was not good reasoning, which I realize now that I understand Him more. He does not *need* anything or anyone to reveal His love for us, but He does give us the example of marriage as one way to understand His love for us.

If God gives us marriage, He will show us how to go about living that life, but He still wants us to love Him more than we love our husband or children. I am not married and don't have children, but even now I have a hard time understanding how I could really follow through on this requirement. When I see the families around me, I realize how much freedom I have to do whatever He requests. Women with families can certainly serve God; in fact, a family can be a huge ministry opportunity. However, everything has its season, and as women who aren't married, we can be unswervingly devoted to God, our relationship with Him, and loving those around us. We have fewer responsibilities in our lives, which makes us more available to go and do whatever God desires. Through honoring God with the time He has given us, our relationship with Him will grow. And this is a relationship that is for eternity.

How Much Does God Want?

Ultimately, we have all been made for our Creator, who instilled in each of us a desire for Him that cannot be filled by anything else. As Blaise Pascal said in *Pensées*, "Man … in vain tries to fill from all his surroundings, seeking from things absent the help he does not obtain in things present[.] But these are all inadequate, because the infinite abyss can only be filled by an infinite and immutable object, that is to say, only by God himself."[14] This "infinite abyss" is sometimes referred to as a God-shaped hole, or a vacuum in our lives that God alone can

---

[14] Blaise Pascal, *Pensées*. Section VII, 425.

fill. Some of us simply do not want to hear about this part of who we are, whereas others accept it but don't know what to do about it. So we get lost, running in vain after things with which to fill this emptiness.

Still others believe this God-shaped hole is only a small, isolated area of our lives. Since our need for God obviously isn't seen as very large, we portion out only a small part of our lives for Him. A. W. Tozer said it well:

> As long as a vessel is filled with something, nothing else can come in … As long as there is something in my life, God cannot fill it. If I empty out half of my life, God can only fill half. And my spiritual life would be diluted with the things of the natural man. This seems to be the condition of many Christians today. They are willing to get rid of some things in their lives, and God comes and fills them as far as He can. But until they are willing to give up everything and put everything on the altar, as it were, God cannot fill their entire lives. One of the strange things about God is that He will come in as far as we allow Him.[15]

Without God, our entire lives are empty. God's single purpose in putting us here on earth was to have a personal, intimate relationship with us. At the beginning of the world, God walked in the garden with Adam and Eve. (See Genesis 3:8–9.) The God of this universe *wanted* to walk and talk with humans. He even sent his Son to earth as a human! (See John 1:1–14.) I can't fathom the love in God's heart for us, which He displayed by sending us Jesus and then the Holy Spirit to dwell in us. (See Romans 8:11.) God wants to be so close to us that His Spirit lives and breathes through our lives. Why would God do this if He wanted only a part of us? No, God wants all of us—our beauty, our mess, our doubts, and our joy. He wants all of us, so that He can let us know all of Him.

---

[15] A. W. Tozer, *The Crucified Life: How to Live Out a Deeper Christian Experience,* p. 54–55.

Watch Out for Side Roads

What Looks Good

We are daily bombarded by advertisements and personal endorsements. People tell us that we *need* to try a particular brand of makeup, supplement, book, social media game, or new relationship. They suggest to us that material things—or personal relationships—can fill the void that we all know is there inside us. But relationships and possessions can so easily lead us off track if we aren't careful about how we prioritize them. We can get lost in an endless cycle of giving ourselves over to possessions or relationships that ultimately prove to be unsatisfying, until we become thoroughly exasperated. Then we give up hope of finding something that will last, and we just settle for anything.

Please don't do this! We must not settle for anything less than Christ in our lives—which is not *settling* at all. But we can't focus on Him if other things and people are blocking our vision, so we need to strip everything else away. A plant can't grow well if weeds grow up around it, and it's the same for us. If we want the good to grow inside us, we need to ask God to help us pull our weeds.

One of my best friends recently experienced heartbreak over a man to whom she had grown close over the years. Their relationship was poorly founded, and my friend knew that she shouldn't have given her heart to him. Their separation was a long and arduous process, because she was letting go of someone whom she had thought would bring her happiness. One day she stumbled across an image on the Internet that depicted a little girl crying as her mother pulled a movie out of her hands. The caption said, "She's crying because I wouldn't buy her the 'dolly' movie." The movie was one of the *Child's Play disk sets*, featuring the evil doll named Chucky. That was particularly meaningful to my friend because she felt like that little girl. God was taking something from her that she had perceived to be good, but actually it wasn't good at all. In her tears she was clinging to this guy, and God was gently pulling him away. She is now grateful that God would not let her keep her "dolly movie."

The world is constantly yelling inside our heads, telling us how to handle these desires, how we should go about finding fulfillment. Our thoughts and, as a result, our actions are so affected by this world that we don't usually realize how much we have bought into its way of thinking. As we are growing up, we start to form a vision for our futures based on the standards of the world around us. But if we narrow our vision to fit the world's standards, we will never understand our true purpose in God. As long as the world remains in its fallen condition, there will always be people around us who do not care about God. Those people won't be able to offer to us good direction for our lives— or even an understanding of what *good* means. Only the Word of God can help us understand what God calls *good* and *evil*, so His Word should always be our guide.

The Bible clearly teaches us to stand apart from the unbelievers around us, "in the world ... not of the world" (John 17:11,16). Many Christians believe we should be able to enjoy the same comforts and pleasures that nonbelievers have. That's the world telling us, "If it looks and sounds good, then it must be good." But God's Word says otherwise: "There is a way which seems right to a man, But its end is the way of death" (Proverbs 14:12).

Not all comforts and pleasures signify "the way of death," but the world telling us that something is right and good doesn't necessarily make it so. God's Word tells us that this life won't always be comfortable, and Paul tells us how his harsh circumstances were used by God for the good of millions of people. (See John 16:33, 2 Corinthians 11:24–27.) God does grant us pleasures in this life, but not necessarily in the ways we have come to expect. In His great wisdom, He will allow things and situations that He calls good, even though our initial reaction to them might be to say, "I don't like this, so it must not be good." God is always looking out for our best interests, whether we agree or not, and we will gradually learn to recognize His goodness in all aspects of our lives. His presence makes hard things not only doable, but even joyful.

Ultimately, however, we should not be focused on this life. When we focus on something, it takes up more of our thoughts, and thus consumes more of our time, and by then our hearts are involved. When we look too long at this world, we start to care only about what is bound to it. But when we look to eternity, we see our present purpose, our eternity with Christ, and everything in between. Also, we will see the importance of using every moment to the glory of God while He has us here.

Temptation

We should run from temptation. We shouldn't just stand there and pray for God to keep us strong. Run! We should run like Joseph did, so fast that he left his shirt behind. (See Genesis 39:12.) In 2 Timothy 2:22, we're told to, "Run from anything that stimulates youthful lusts. Instead, pursue righteous living, faithfulness, love and peace" (NLT).

I remember a friend talking to me about a guy she liked even though she knew deep down he wasn't good for her. She would let herself get into compromising situations with him, as though she believed she could handle it. I used to watch movies with sexual content, thinking I could handle seeing people partially clothed and passionately making out. At the time, I didn't realize—or want to realize—the effect those movies had on my thought life and passionate desires. I was playing with temptation, thinking, *I can handle this*. I didn't run from it, because I thought I could tame it. How foolish! It wasn't until years later that I started to recognize that I was in bondage to a sexually inappropriate thought life.

Anything that can provoke us to sin is a temptation, but temptation itself is not sinful. Only when we choose to act on temptation—whether in thought, word, or behavior—does it lead to sin. I used to think the word *temptation* applied only to things that invoke lust or greed, but temptation isn't reserved for only the "major" sins. It also can apply to many other situations in life. For instance, the idea of a comfortable life can be a temptation that takes hold of us and causes us to sin.

A few years ago, when I was trying to figure out where God wanted me to live, I had the choice between a city with very strong Christian roots and a city that did not seem to care about God. The comfort side of me wanted to live in the Christian environment, because that's how I grew up, but I knew from previous experience that if I lived there, I would be tempted into complacency. It's easy for me to just fall in line with other people when they are doing what seems culturally correct and doesn't contradict the easy scriptures that I feel like following. But I knew I couldn't really pick and choose what parts of God's Word I wanted to believe; I had to accept the whole of scripture.

So I ended up choosing the city in which I knew I would stand out. I wanted to live wholly dependent on God and not allow myself to be swayed by an easy Christian culture. That might not have been the right choice for everyone, but it was right for me at the time. I believe that having to make that decision, at that time of my life, was a test to see where my heart was. Was I thirsting for the Lord and the comfort found only in Him, or was I looking for earthly comfort? To this day I am thankful that the Holy Spirit opened my eyes to this knowledge of my nature, and He is daily giving me the strength to live for Him.

When we run from temptation, we should run toward the Father who never gives his children stones instead of bread. (See Matthew 7:9.) When we run to God for safety, He will be our strong tower. (See Psalm 61:3.) When we run to Him for freedom, He will break our chains. (See Psalm 107:14.) When we run to Him and lay our lives down at His feet in surrender, He will give us Himself, the true fulfillment of our lives.

Our Time, His Time

Another way we block ourselves from experiencing true fulfillment is by staying busy, even in doing things that don't take much effort. We don't like complete silence and stillness. Empty time makes us uneasy. We want to be out doing things with our friends, or at home watching TV or reading a book. But sometimes true fulfillment is found in the silence of God's presence. Being still and silent before the Lord is beautiful and fulfilling.

It can also be a challenge and, honestly, one of the hardest lessons to really learn well in this day and age. First, we must find the right time and place. Then our task is to quiet our minds and empty ourselves so that He can fill us up. We must be poured out like an offering before the Lord. When we offer our lives, He will fill us with His Spirit, love, joy, and complete and perfect peace. We should not minimize the importance of this lesson of silence and stillness, which is the true beginning of intimacy with God. It is a challenge, but one worthy of our effort.

Will It Last?

Everything done through the Lord's strength and guidance will last, but anything that we do outside the will of God will fade away to nothing. (See 1 Corinthians 3:12–14.) God's Word will last forever. (See Matthew 24:35.) The things He calls into being will stand forever. God is eternal, the only fulfillment that will last. Jesus says in John 6:35, "I am the bread of life; he who comes to Me will not hunger, and he who believes in Me will never thirst." "Whoever drinks of the water that I will give him shall never thirst; but the water that I will give him will become in him a well of water springing up to eternal life" (John 4:14).

God is our eternal source of satisfaction, but we have to believe. The best way to actively believe is not only to read and know His Word for us in the Bible, but to use His words to combat our daily thoughts that result from the influence of the environment in which we live. For instance, the environment around me tells me I am not living a fulfilled life because I do not have a husband, I don't have kids, or I'm not doing something amazingly great for the world. Yet God's Word says, "It will no longer be said to you, 'Forsaken,' Nor to your land will it any longer be said, 'Desolate'; But you will be called, 'My delight is in her,' And your land, 'Married'; For the Lord delights in you, and to Him your land will be married ... And you will be called, 'Sought out, a city not forsaken" (Isaiah 62: 4, 12).

"'It will come about in that day,' declares the Lord, 'That you will call Me Ishi [husband] and will no longer call Me Baali [my master]'" (Hosea 2:16; clarification added).

Fulfillment comes through living for Him, following His example, seeking Him above all other relationships. This kind of fulfillment never fails, and God wants to be this for us. He longs for us and is waiting for us to choose Him wholeheartedly.

True Fulfillment and the Single Woman

While coming to a place of surrender to God in the area of relationships, I have learned more about who God is and how much He loves me. Only through understanding this better have come to a place of peace with not having a physical husband. I still have times when I struggle with this issue, but God has made it much better than it was before. When I am struggling with feeling alone or unfulfilled, I shift my focus. I stop thinking about what I don't have, and focus instead on what I *do* have. I have a loving Father who is always giving me His best. (See James 1:17.) I have a brother, Jesus, who is always interceding on my behalf. (See Hebrews 7:25.) And I have the Holy Spirit, who is always with me, speaking life, hope, and love over me. (See John 6:63, Romans 15:13, Romans 5:5.) God is never far away, regardless of my emotions at any particular time. He is always working things out for my good. I believe this, and I trust Him more than ever.

I do not always feel satisfied, but when this happens, I know I need to spend more time with God or go out and love someone else. Either way, if I am feeling unsatisfied, I know I have allowed myself to focus on a lie. (He isn't enough. He doesn't care. I don't have what others have or what I desire right now. It's supposed to be all about me. And so on.) The sooner I realize where my mind and eyes are focused, the sooner I'm able to redirect them back to Jesus and His love for me. This is an important lesson, which I continue to work on today.

7

THE FOCUS OF DREAMS

One thing I have asked from the Lord,
that I shall seek:
That I may dwell in the house of the Lord
all the days of my life,
To behold the beauty of the Lord
And to meditate in His temple.
For in the day of trouble He will conceal
Me in His tabernacle;
In the secret place of His tent He will hide me;
He will lift me up on a rock.

—Psalm 27:4–5

Before we start to talk about our dreams, I want to clarify a few words and the way I will be using them. In general, I think of a promise of God as something that points to His character. Normally the promises that we have been given in His Word are about what He will do in, through, or for us. These promises range from providing our needs to giving us His righteousness. He will do these things faithfully, but we will be steadily learning how He will do them or what they will look like in our lives. Promises such as His righteousness will be the same for everyone, but some of the other promises, such as provision, might be different for different people. For each of us, God meets our needs and works in us in personal and unique ways.

When I use the word *dream*, I'm referring to God-given desires or

97

understandings about what He wants to do in our daily and future lives. God does speak to us in personal ways, but sometimes we don't hear His words because they seem so normal and natural. Yet at other times He will speak in very large, bold ways that will definitely get our attention.

At the outset of this discussion of dreams, I do want to make one thing clear. If we ever look forward to our dreams more than to God, then we have put our dreams in the place of God. We have taken Him off His throne in our lives and substituted something infinitely inferior. Our hearts too easily give more importance to the things we see before us in life, which often have very little eternal significance. With this understanding, let's begin.

Dreams from Whom?

From whom do our dreams come? Most people do not hesitate when asked this question. Until a few years ago, I would have answered, "From me, of course." The idea of anyone else giving me a dream for my life was not only foreign to me, but did not sit well. I have a tendency to be stubborn and rebellious, not wanting to do what other people tell me to do—which is something I am sure God will continue to work out of me. So I would have immediately rejected the idea of someone else giving me a dream, especially a major life dream. But after much surrender and attitude adjustment through the power of the Holy Spirit, I can say that when I truly desire to live in God's light and walk in His ways, the dreams that mean anything to me will come from Him.

We all have dreams for our lives, but most of them come and go. They hold value for a time, at least in our own hearts and minds, but usually they don't last, just like everything else in this life. If we want a dream that will last into eternity, we must cling to our God and King, our only hope of a full future, and tell Him we aren't letting go until He blesses us with a future.

That's what Jacob did in the scriptures, when he wrestled with the man all night until he was given a blessing. Let's begin in the middle of Jacob's story, after Jacob sent his family and belongings on ahead, as he was getting closer to meeting his brother Esau:

> Then Jacob was left alone, and a man wrestled with him until daybreak. When he [the man] saw that he had not prevailed against him [Jacob], he touched the socket of his thigh; so the socket of Jacob's thigh was dislocated while he wrestled with him. Then he said, "Let me go, for the dawn is breaking." But he [Jacob] said, "I will not let you go unless you bless me." So he said to him, "What is your name?" And he said, "Jacob." He said, "Your name shall no longer be Jacob, but Israel; for you have striven with God and with men and have prevailed." (Genesis 32:24; clarification added)

Most people come at this story the wrong way, as I did for years. They think that it was out of pride, or because he saw it as his right, that Jacob made his request—or demand, really—for God to bless him. But one night, the Holy Spirit helped me understand this, and now I see Jacob's story differently. Why would God bless a prideful person who came to Him out of a sense of entitlement and demanded a blessing? In many scriptures, God disapproves of proud people. (See Leviticus 26:19; Proverbs 3:34, 16:5; Isaiah 13:11; James 4:6.)

Jacob wasn't proud—he was at the end of his rope. In the verses right before this story of him wrestling with someone, we see a broken Jacob, scared for his life and the lives of everyone in his family. He was about to meet his brother Esau, who was bringing four hundred men with him. That would intimidate anyone. But to make matters worse, the last time Jacob had been with Esau, he had stolen his father Isaac's blessing from Esau and taken it for himself. Now God had told Jacob to go back to Canaan, where Esau, who had every right to be angry with Jacob, was coming out to meet him with four hundred men. Yikes! Out of fear, Jacob decided to divide his family into groups, hoping that even if one group was killed, another group might survive.

That was Jacob's situation—mentally, emotionally, and physically—when an unnamed man appeared on the scene. Scripture tells us that the man had authority to give Jacob a blessing from God, so the man could have been Jesus, an angel, or some other representative of God. When the man arrived, Jacob recognized his authority to grant God's blessing, and he clung to the man out of desperation—not because of pride or a sense of entitlement.

Through the night, God tested Jacob about how much he really needed God's blessing and His presence. God seemed to wait all night so that Jacob could learn the depth of his need, and to let Jacob decide to whom he would completely trust his life. Even after Jacob was wounded, he still didn't give up on what God could do in him and through him, even though it was God who injured him. Wow, that bears repeating … Even though God, through the unnamed man, gave Jacob an injury that would last the rest of his life, Jacob did not lose faith in God. He accepted the wound as God's choice for his life. He didn't go off and cry, but he held on tight, knowing that God was his only hope.

Because Jacob held on to God for His salvation and deliverance, God blessed him with a life dream, a promise, and a covenant that was passed down from Abraham. God also gave Jacob a new name, and he gave Jacob and his family a future. When Jacob was worried about living through the next day, God gave him a future that would last through generations into eternity. Jacob might have limped for the rest of his life, as a reminder of his encounter with God, but his life was blessed by the Creator of the universe.

We need to remember where we stand, when it comes to demanding things from God. We should never approach God in pride and demand things of Him. Instead, we should go to his throne in humility and boldness, knowing He is our Father, and lay our requests at His feet. Jacob didn't just impulsively say to God, "Hey, I want a dream and blessing, so I'm not letting go till you do what I want." He actually said something like this: "God, You told me to come here. And yet without Your help, I will not survive. So I'm holding on to You, my only hope!

Bless me!" Jacob didn't run and hide, and he didn't go back to what he knew and where he had previously felt safe. He clung to God and continued in the direction he was told to go.

Focus of the Heart

When we think of life dreams, what comes to mind are usually things we want to do with our lives—anything from visiting another country to wanting to have a ministry that helps millions of people. Life dreams can be good and even God centered, but they usually are no more focused on God than we already are in our daily lives. To what extent have we surrendered to the will of God? How do our daily lives prove our love for God? Are we living completely for His honor in the normal things of life, or are we waiting for God to give us something *big* to do for Him? We have a tendency to desire only things that look good or important, but God is joyous when we honor Him in the small, daily things of life. And actually I believe these small, *normal* things can often bring Him more pride in us as His children than the things which look big.

The closer to God I come, the more I realize that my life dreams have been selfish. I've wanted to do things for others, but I've also wanted to gain something from it—a good feeling from doing something nice, recognition from others, or pride in myself for being a good person. I generally didn't have in mind the concept of being "poured out as a drink offering" (Philippians 2:17), or else I probably would have run in the other direction.

I actually did run from complete commitment to God for many years. I had been taught from an early age to serve others with my life, but I also wanted to be comfortable doing so. I wasn't at the place where I really desired God's will above my own. I had not really paid attention to His love for me, and therefore I did not love Him fully in return. Because of this, I could not bring myself to love God enough to surrender all my wants and dreams to His wisdom.

God doesn't require us to surrender to Him, but we know from His Word and actions that He cares for us and loves us passionately. (See 1 Peter 5:7.) If He weren't perfect in *everything,* then we would be wrong to give our everything to Him, but Matthew tells us that our heavenly Father is perfect in all things. (See Matthew 5:48.) Sometimes we're asked to surrender parts of our lives to God before we really know much about Him, which requires us to take a step of faith. We don't always see what God sees or know what He knows, and as our knowledge of Him grows, He will give us bigger and bigger situations that will require even more faith. When we trust that He has our best interests in mind, He will move us forward in life to bring Himself glory. Even if we don't see the results during our lifetime, God will not let anything we do for Him be lost. He will establish the work of our hands. (See Psalm 90:17.)

I am learning this in my daily walk with Him. He is teaching me more of who He is, His ways, and how my faith in Him is growing. I know that with every step I take, I am learning to love and trust Him more, and with this I am pleasing His heart.

If we want to live in His light and truly receive salvation, we must give God our all. Believing that Jesus died for our sins, yet not obeying Him and what He tells us to do, is not true salvation. If we think that getting to heaven requires absolutely nothing of us beyond just accepting Christ, that's pseudo-salvation. God clearly says we must obey Him. (See John 3:36.) We don't have the option of saying to Him, "Maybe if You do this, God, then I will do that." We can't put Him off by saying, "When it's convenient for me, God, then I'll obey You."

People who refuse to give God every area of their lives are even worse off than those who are not saved through Jesus Christ. (See 2 Peter 2:20.) They have deceived themselves into thinking they love God, but they do not even know Him. Love that doesn't involve intimate knowledge is artificial love or, at best, weak love that is not guaranteed to stand through times of testing. We must be actively seeking Him and His glory for this love to be anything of worth. If we truly knew Him, we would run to Him like lost children coming home to their father's arms. We would give Him everything—no questions asked, no bargaining—for He is good! When we, in our weakness, do not understand God, He, in His love, still understands us.

Can We Build Our Dreams?

"A man's heart plans his ways, but the Lord directs his steps" (Proverbs 16:9 NKJV). God has given us the ingenuity to create and plan out our days, but too many people ignore the last part of this verse. They think, *I can do whatever I want, or at least what looks good to me.* But God's logic and ours often do not match. We think that when we plan our ways, as long as they don't contradict what we're told in the Bible, that God will bless our choices. Sometimes this is true, but it is also true that just because something looks good or is attainable doesn't mean it is godly.

"There is a way which seems right to a man, but its end is the way of death" (Proverbs 14:12). This verse is sobering. Even when something looks right, according to God it might not be. We could find ourselves on a path leading to death, because we're blinded by our desires and the influences around us. We should always be on alert, checking what we think and do against what God wants, as conveyed to us in scripture and revealed through our relationship with Him.

Furthermore, not everything permitted by the world around us is truly profitable to us as Christians. (See 1 Corinthians 6:12.) In our country, we have certain legal rights and freedoms, but that doesn't mean those would be holy choices for us. Even here, God's Word supersedes all other laws.

Making dreams without God's direction is a recipe for failure. How many of us have started with a dream, just to see it fail? Or we get to the end of a dream and realize that it has no lasting worth? Sometimes we have dreams that don't last for more than a day. Are these not disheartening? A part of us dies when our dreams die.

After years of dreams that went nowhere, I became disheartened and bitter. A poisoned well, I was angry at God. In the book of Ruth, we have the story of Naomi, who changed her name to Mara, meaning *bitter*, when her future was stripped away from her. (See Ruth 1:20.) She thought God had abandoned her, when actually He was working a bigger plan than she could have imagined. He was going to give Naomi a new future through the life of Ruth. Sometimes we get so focused on our own dreams that we neglect to widen our vision to God's dreams for us.

Let's remind ourselves of a couple of things. God does speak promises to us in His Word and throughout our lives. He gives us direction about what He wants us to do and how we should live, and He gives us a purpose to work toward. But we must be careful about how we view the dreams, direction, and purpose that we get from God. First, we must never let anything take precedence over God in our lives. Also, we must be careful not to look at God as our personal genie or fortune-teller, even though He loves to give us dreams and reveal His purpose for our lives. Ultimately, our focus should be solely on loving and serving Him. From this, everything else will have its proper place in our lives—and I mean *everything*.

It can be hard to understand why we have to wait for the Lord's words to come true, but sometimes He delays so that we can see how much we really want Him and whether we desire Him more than the things that He's promised to us. At other times, He is still developing us into a person who will handle well the vision He has for us. God cares for us and wants us to be amazing where He puts us, and sometimes this takes a lot of preparation. The promises He gives us might not even come to fruition in our lifetime. Think of all the men and women mentioned in Hebrews 11. They did not see in their lifetime the fulfillment of the promises God gave them, yet we here today are that fulfillment.

Many times we simply have to wait for God's timing to be right, which can take years. Abraham had to wait more than twenty years before God's promise to him of a son was fulfilled, even though God personally called Abraham a friend. (See Genesis 12:4, 7, 21:5; James 2:23.) Even after He gave Abraham a son, God tested him by asking Abraham to give his son *back* to God. God didn't test Abraham so that He could know Abraham's heart—He wanted Abraham to know his own heart. God knows the hearts of all people, but we often do not know ourselves, so He brings these times of testing to remind us to focus on Him. We can see by this story that God cares deeply about how much we desire Him and where He is placed in our lives.

The story of Abraham offers another lesson that we need to take to heart. Just because God tells us about a promise He will give us, that does not mean He needs our help in bringing it about. We do not want an Ishmael like Abraham and Sarah received by attempting to help God keep His promise. (See Genesis 16.) Everything has its timing and season in God. (See Genesis 21:2, Ecclesiastes 3:1.) God wants to guide our lives, but we must give Him control. It's like the song "In Over My Head" by Jenn Johnson and John-Paul Gentile says: "Then You crash over me and I've lost control but I'm free."

We have been raised in a "name it, claim it" culture, which was never God's plan. It's true that when we are battling against the Enemy, we need to stand on the promises of God, and sometimes when we have gone deeper in knowing God, He tells us to claim His gifts in our lives or for others. But we must be careful not to demand things from God or tell Him how He should fulfill His promises in our lives. We need to let God be God.

More than eight years ago, while sleeping God gave me a dream in which I saw my future husband and, as a result, experienced a feeling of complete peace which I had rarely experienced at this point in my life. Yet as time went on and the dream wasn't fulfilled, I became hurt and confused. I felt God wasn't being true to His promise, and I would sometimes throw it in His face and complain about it not being fulfilled. I wondered if He was punishing me or had forgotten me, or maybe the dream wasn't really from Him in the first place.

Since then I've realized that I had put God's promise on my own timeline and molded it to what I thought would be good. Without asking God about the meaning of this dream, I had established my own expectations about it. All I saw was the altar and my future husband standing next to it. I had jumped headlong into believing that one day soon, God would give me the man from the dream, and I had grasped this dream so tightly that there was no room for God. Now I believe God was using the dream to give me hope and draw me closer to Him. I believe now He was the groom in my dream. This is something I wasn't able to grasp at the time of the dream, but since has begun to make perfect sense.   God can use every challenge to bring us closer to Him, whether it's waiting for something He has promised or the silence when we do not hear Him. When we have a strong desire that isn't being fulfilled, we can hear Him saying, "How much do you want Me? Do you desire that other thing more than you desire Me?" And when we don't sense Him close, He is really saying, "Press into Me. Am I not good? Am I not everything you want or need? Will you come closer, even when everything around you is screaming I'm not there? Your feelings will lie to you. Who are you listening to, Me and My Word or your feelings?"

Our hearts can have only one king, and until we choose Him, we will never be at peace. It's time to awaken our hearts to His. It's time to see that God is good and that He will never give us a desire that doesn't point to Him in some way. If we're angry at God or mourning a desire that hasn't been filled, then we should ask ourselves, "How much have I really surrendered to Him? How much is He worth to me? Is my God good?"

God does not make empty promises. He is a man of His word. If something is of God, He will see it done. He does not let anything that He speaks into being fall to the ground. (See Isaiah 55:11.) His words are true and life giving. He created the whole earth—everything we see, feel, hear, smell, and touch—by *speaking*, and that is still how His words work in our lives today. (See Genesis 1.)

What Is Our Focus?

I want to preface the next three sections by saying that if I come across as yelling or demanding to know what you are doing, it's because my heart cries out for everyone to know a loving relationship with God. Please take these next three sections as a cry from a heart longing for you to fall more deeply in love with the lover of your soul.

God cares more deeply for us than we can know. He knows how many hairs are on our heads. (See Luke 12:7.) He loves us and even *likes* us. But we become distracted by the business of life, which deafens us to the sound of His voice calling us out of our sin and closer to Him, deaf to His direction in our lives, deaf to His love to us and everything He wants for us. Being unable to hear God's voice puts us in a scary place.

I hope and pray that the Holy Spirit will speak to your heart and mind, and awaken you to the reality of where you are. Maybe you are a long way from God, or maybe you have only a few things here and there that are not completely given to the Lord. We all have room for growth in our relationship with God, which is never meant to be stagnant. We are always meant to be "falling forward," as Gary Thomas says.[16]

His Voice

Sometimes we get so lost in what *could* be that we forget to focus on God and what He says *should* be. God will not always break into our daily lives and tell us not to do this or that, but He often guides us with little whispered suggestions. God wants us to be sensitive to Him. Can He interrupt our lives? Can we hear or recognize Him when He speaks? He gives us the freedom to live our own lives, but He wants to

---

[16] Gary L. Thomas, *Sacred Marriage*, p. 154.

be intimately involved. And He wants us to desire His involvement so much that we are sensitive to His direction, even if it's a whisper.

God can create an earthquake that topples our world, or He can speak to us in a quiet whisper. Sometimes God allows times of illness or great need in our lives to bring us closer to Him and reveal His grace. But instead of turning toward God in such times, we often respond by becoming angry or depressed, or by simply feeling overwhelmed. So if we don't notice the earthquake, how likely are we to notice the whisper? How can we truly walk in God's direction and live our lives according to His will unless we become more sensitive to His voice? Can we truly build our dreams with His guidance, without knowing who He really is or what His heart desires? How can we say we are doing what God wants for our lives when we don't even recognize His voice?

Our Time Is Short

We take into the future only what we have started to work toward today. Did we accept Jesus just to get to heaven, or do we want more? I have a hard time believing that God intends nothing more than simply to let us in the gates of heaven. Why would God sacrifice His Son so that we can live with Him forever, if we don't really love Him or want to spend our lives getting to know Him? The little time we have here on earth is nothing compared with eternity, so we have only a short time to learn about God before we find ourselves standing before His face. When that happens, do we want our hearts set on earthly things or on Him? God's heart desperately wants us, now *and* for eternity.

Unfortunately, many of us think we have plenty of time to develop our relationship with God . We tell ourselves, "Tomorrow I'll make a strong effort to know Jesus." Or, "Tomorrow I'll give up my bad habits and instead really seek God." But we are not guaranteed tomorrow. Life is as brief as a wisp of smoke, and we shouldn't put off something this important for an unknown tomorrow. Our relationship with God shouldn't wait for tomorrow. To postpone choosing Him is a sure way to be caught off guard and set ourselves up for failure.

What if we put it off so long that we forget what we were supposed to be doing? Many Christians have forgotten their call from God. They have allowed daily life to distract them and quiet the call of God to walk in His love and purpose. Instead, we want to be comfortable and happy, but we will pay a heavy price for this. Our choices have consequences. God will forgive sins, but that does not mean He will always removed sin's consequences.

Were we created to enjoy a powerful relationship with the God of the universe or to live a mediocre life? I don't believe we can really love God and live mediocre lives. If our lives are full of God's presence, they will be extraordinary. If He isn't present in how we love others and we aren't learning to be more like Him, then we are not yet loving Him fully and thus His power is not really free to work in and through us.

Let us not waste the precious time we have. We should take now, every moment, and search with all our hearts, minds, and spirits for the King of glory. What is our focus?

His Yoke

Jesus says that His yoke is easy and light, but most of God's children don't have His yoke around their necks at all. (See Matthew 11:30.) Many people accept Jesus's salvation, but then continue to do whatever they want, rather than doing what Jesus wants. When we live this way, instead of taking His yoke which is easy and light, we have taken one for ourselves that is as heavy as iron. Our yoke is like iron because we still are trying to live the way we want, even though God has called us to live a higher life in Him. If we do this we have assumed that salvation gives us liberty to do whatever we want, without the need to surrender our desires to God. We say we are living for Him, but we aren't willing to let Him examine the depths of our hearts to root out the impurities.

We need to stop deceiving ourselves. The work Christ did on the cross does not equal our obedience. If we aren't fully surrendered to Jesus and His Spirit working in our lives, then we aren't carrying the yoke that He intended to share with us. We are making things complicated by refusing to give Him every aspect of our lives, but we can't have it both ways if we want to fully experience God. The idea of surrendering everything to God can be frightening, and a part of us really doesn't want to give up control. However, giving God control doesn't mean we become His puppets. God won't take away our free will, but we can choose to value what He wants above what we originally thought was important. We can learn to care more about what He desires, as the lover of our souls. By giving Him control, we make ourselves open and attentive to what God is telling us in every area of our lives.

This can be hard, because our desire for control is usually very strong. But surrendering to God is so beautiful that it can't be explained—it has to be lived. There is peace and freedom here that we will not find anywhere else.

When we have learned to focus our lives on God, we will truly see and comprehend the dreams He has for us. This is not always easy, but when we choose to come back again and again to Him and surrender to His Omniscience, then we gain the peace and comfort that only He can give.

Dream Big

God has amazing plans for us! "'For I know the plans that I have for you,' declares the Lord, 'plans for welfare and not for calamity to give you a future and a hope'" (Jeremiah 29:11). The next few verses in Jeremiah tell us how God will go about providing us a future and a hope. "'You will seek Me and find Me when you search for me with all your heart. I will be found by you,' declares the Lord, 'and I will restore your fortunes and will gather you from all the nations and from all the places where I have driven you'" (Jeremiah 29:13–14).

Verses 13 and 14 are important to our understanding of verse 11. God's plans for us, as described in verse 11, are conditional. He wants to provide a future and a hope for us, but first He says, "You will *seek* Me" (emphasis added). When we do this with *all* our hearts, He will be found by us. Then, while this is being done, He will provide our future.

The value we put on the things we do is also important. Just because a dream looks like something God might want, that doesn't mean it's exactly what He wants for us. He will give us a big dream, yet it might not come in the form that we expect. Being a mother is a *big* dream— one of the hardest jobs in the whole world to do well, and one of the most important. In contrast, doing service without other people seeing or knowing about it might seem small and insignificant, but nothing is small or unimportant when God has commissioned us to do it.

Unfortunately, often we cannot see the true value of our work. Our measure of importance is influenced by the standards of the world around us. But we must remember that whatever we do, we are doing it for God. What greater honor? Because our whole lives are set apart as holy to God, everything we do is an offering to the Lord, whether a worthy one or an unworthy one. Whether we complain or experience joy, it's an offering to Him. Do we want to complain to the King of Kings and Lord of Lords that He didn't give us a sufficiently important dream?

The disciples argued about who would be greater in heaven, and when the mother of two disciples asked for a more honored place for her sons in heaven, Jesus said, "You do not know what you are asking. Are you able to drink the cup that I am about to drink?" (Matthew 20:22). If they wanted to be great, the disciples had to be willing to serve like Jesus did, even to the cross. Jesus also said that to be great in the kingdom of heaven, we must be a servant to all: "But Jesus called them to Himself and said, 'You know that the rulers of the Gentiles lord it over them, and their great men exercise authority over them. It is not this way among you, but whoever wishes to become great among you shall be your servant, and whoever wishes to be first among you shall be your slave; just as the Son of Man did not come to be served, but to serve, and to give His life a ransom for many'" (Matthew 20:25–28).

To gain a higher place in the kingdom of God, we have to be more like Jesus and possess a servant's heart. In the preceding passage from Matthew, Jesus shows us that His view of what is great and the world's view of what is great are exactly opposite. He wants us to do all things for Him with joy, even when we're called to be a slave to all. This pure form of dying to self is not easy and doesn't come to anyone naturally. Only through Jesus can we have the power and humility—much less the desire—to walk this life.

God desires great things for us! Paul says in 1 Corinthians 2:9–10, "'No eye has seen, no ear has heard, no mind has conceived what God has prepared for those who love him'—but God has revealed it to us by His Spirit" (NIV). Paul is speaking not only about our eternal futures that God has prepared for us, but also about our lives right now. Through the Holy Spirit, we can start to understand and experience God's plans for us. The Holy Spirit will change not only our outlook, but our whole lives. The scriptures tell us to ask God, our Father, to give us the Holy Spirit. Jesus says in Luke 11:13, "If you then, being evil, know how to give good gifts to your children, how much more will your heavenly Father give the Holy Spirit to those who ask Him?" Jesus is assuring us that God will give the Holy Spirit to His children when they ask.

With the Holy Spirit, we can have the boldness to dream big. Because of the Holy Spirit's wisdom and guidance, we will see and understand God's dreams for our lives. Through the Holy Spirit, we can beautifully live out God's dreams for our lives. But of all our dreams, God longs to be the biggest.

8

How to Love the World as a Single Woman

You are the sun shining down on everyone
Light of the world giving light to everything I see
Beauty so brilliant I can hardly take it in
And everywhere you are is warmth and light

And I am the moon with no light of my own
Still you have made me to shine
And as I glow in this cold dark night
I know I can't be a light unless I turn my face to you
—Sara Groves, *"You Are the Sun"*

This is challenging for me. I do love people, but not always in a patient or coddling way. Hurting for people and their situations in life, I look for ways to help them, but I have a tendency to expect people to learn from their choices or the choices of those around them. Maintaining compassion and love for people when they keep making poor choices is hard for me. I have to often pray, "Lord, may You give me a heart of compassion for others, and may the love I have for You grow and spill over into my love for the people around me, whether they know You or not." I feel the love of Christ for others only if He first gives it to me. If I am to show His love, I need to abide in His love so it can overflow to the world around me.

"For God so loved the world, that He gave His only begotten Son, that whoever believes in Him shall not perish but have eternal life"

(John 3:16). This is a well-known verse, but that does not lessen the heart of it. Not only did God create us, but He also knew when He created this world that He was going to have to die for us. Before He created the world, He chose to love us enough to die for us. Let this sink in ... No greater love exists. God loves us and wants His love to shine through us to the world. Jesus was lifted up on a hill so that the world could witness His death and, through Him, God's love for all. Likewise we are to be that light on a hill, reflecting forever the light of God's love for those around us today. We are His ambassadors. We are daughters of the King, sent to reflect God's beauty and love for the world to see.

Where Do We Start?

When I have learnt to love God better than my earthly dearest, I shall love my earthly dearest better than I do now.
—C. S. Lewis, *Letters of C. S. Lewis*

The only way to start loving others is by loving the Lord. Even though we think we love Him, we are often blind to the fact that we don't even know Him. To grow in love for our God, we must spend time with Him—personal, intimate, face-to-face time. Our hearts must desire to love Him and seek His face. We must learn to love Him more than anything, ourselves included. And we can simply but sincerely ask Him to help us love Him more, which is a request He will always answer. This is the beginning, not the end, of how to walk with the Lord.

I was raised in a Christian family, and I am thankful God placed me in this loving and nurturing family. But as I grew up, I adopted my parents' beliefs and parroted them in my own life without establishing my own daily relationship with God. I had not made Him my own. I told myself, "I talk to God with almost every thought. In fact, I'm probably talking to Him more than the people around me think that

I should." I really did desire God in my life and I wanted to be used by Him, but I was lazy and unwilling to make a daily commitment to Him. I was lazy. I thought that reading my Bible occasionally and talking with Him in my thoughts made me "good."

I did not really understand God's profound love for me, and had not taken the words *God loves me* to heart. Occasionally I got a glimpse of His love, which would lead me to a mountaintop experience in which I was on fire for God, but then my memory of His love would fail me and I would slip back into confusion and wandering. I found myself relying on other people's strength and relationships with God to guide me and give me hope, but I still wasn't willing to choose God above the laziness and ease I craved. I wanted more of God in my life, but He asked too much in return. I was comfortable as a stagnant Christian, and I didn't want to put any more effort into a relationship I could not understand. In retrospect, I think the real problem was my lack of understanding about God's deep, all-covering, life-giving, empowering, peaceful, passionate love for me. God's abiding love is always with me, no matter what I feel or think.

One day, God basically gave me an ultimatum: "It's you or me. Who are you going to choose?" I had faint memories of being taught about God many years earlier, but no recent experience with Him to inform my choice—although I did realize the emptiness of my life without Him. My years of wandering had taught me a lot about my true nature and how easily I ran toward sin. I knew that Jesus was my only way back to the heart of God, and so, in a step of faith and desperation, I chose Jesus. Finally deciding to truly seek a relationship with God, I allowed Him to cleanse me of my unrighteousness.

After I spent a good deal of time on my knees in repentance, my passion for God was burning bright. I realized that He needs to be my daily priority, which means setting aside devoted time every day for Him. I am not a morning person, but I want to carry God's perspective with me throughout my day, which means focusing my heart on Him at the beginning of the day. I want Him from beginning to end, and even in my dreams. I don't like getting up early, but God is worth more than my sleep. At first this was tough, but now I enjoy getting up early if I know that means I get to spend that much more time with Him. I have found that unless I make Him my habit, other things will take His place. God should be my most important habit, thoroughly ingrained into my life—a habit built not on duty, but on the understanding of how much I need Him and how much He loves me.

Our daily habit of God should involve consistent interaction with Him in a variety of ways. As we develop deeper intimacy with God, He will show us His ways and how to walk in them. He will open our eyes to the needs around us and get our focus off of ourselves. When we focus on Him, He gives us vision to see the world around us for what it really is, what its purpose is, and how He wants us to help it.

Where We Get Caught

We are to be in the world, not of the world. Until we take this to heart, we will never understand the extent to which we have become influenced and affected by the world. We will not see how much we need transformation in Christ. The first step is recognizing our need to be changed. We are a people of hard hearts and selfish ways, and if we refuse to change, we will never have the freedom of walking in God's perfect ways or experience His peace that goes beyond understanding. (See Jeremiah 16:12.)

In Jeremiah 11:15–16 God says to His people, "'What right has My beloved in My house when she has done vile deeds? Can the sacrificial flesh take away from you your disaster, so that you can rejoice?' The Lord called your name, 'A green olive tree, beautiful in fruit and form'; with the noise of a great tumult He has kindled fire on it, and its branches are worthless.'" Jeremiah, a prophet of God, was speaking to the Jewish people. They were already set apart as God's beloved, just as we are, but they were not serving Him. Instead, they were serving their own selfish desires and doing "vile deeds."

God will have none of this. When we do things that don't meet the standard of the Spirit of God, we defile ourselves. No amount of coming to God with sacrificial money, time, or service for the Lord will heal our depravity, unless we come in repentance and turn from our unholy and selfish ways. Obeying God in the first place is far better than disobeying Him and then trying to make up for it. (See 1 Samuel 15:22.) God wants us to be "beautiful in fruit and form." If we do not give up the ways of the world around us and live our lives set apart for holiness, He will be angered into kindling a fire against His beloved and calling the things we do in life worthless. Let us turn from our selfishness and depravity, which has been in us from birth and reinforced by the world, before that happens.

We tend to think that to serve the world, we need to look relevant to it. We think that people will listen to us only if we blend in, but this is not true. It's fine to wear trendy clothes or a popular hairstyle, as long as we don't talk and act like the world. We can honor God while enjoying cultural trends, as long as they don't violate His holiness.

In his biography of St. Thomas Aquinas, G. K. Chesterton says, "Therefore it is the paradox of history that each generation is converted by the saint who contradicts it most."[17] Because of Jesus's amazing sacrifice, we already are saints and members of the royal priesthood. (See 1 Corinthians 1:2, 1 Peter 2:10.) We are to be holy as God is holy, and we shouldn't compromise His holiness in us by trying to be relevant or to fit in. It isn't our similarities with our culture that will draw people to God, but our differences. When we compromise by not showing God's holiness in our lives, we lose the very ground we hoped to gain for Christ in other people's lives. The world is looking for people who are completely devoted to the Lord and actually live the way they preach. When people see the sincerity, power, and love that is

---

[17] G. K. Chesterton, *St. Thomas Aquinas*, p. 424.

born and cultivated by living in God's life, many will be drawn to His heart shining through us.

Jesus was a man apart and our ultimate example of how to live. The disciples did not blend in; they were men set apart to follow Christ, and we are to follow in their example. We are to live our lives holy and pure, free of any form or habit that resembles the sin of this world. People are thirsty for Jesus, whether they realize it or not. Jesus says, "He who believes in Me, as the Scripture said, 'From his innermost being will flow rivers of living water'" (John 7:38). We must remain crystal clear so that we can bring His refreshing and living water to the people in our lives.

Will It Be Easy?

Jesus told us that when we are living holy lives in a corrupt world, the world will hate us. "Because you are not of the world, but I chose you out of the world, because of this the world hates you" (John 15:19). In our society, we experience subtle persecution against our Christian beliefs, such as when someone rolls their eyes at the mention of church or makes ugly comments about one of their Christian friends. Our elected officials are also passing more laws that constrict Christianity, such as taking God out of our courtrooms, public buildings, and schools. If our government strays further from the biblical foundation on which the United States of America was established, we can be guaranteed that the persecution we Christians face for living holy lives for God will increase.

As we face daily persecution by the world, what is our response? Do we become angry at those tearing us down? Do we hide who Jesus is to us? Or do we take these opportunities to love our enemies and continue being lights in this dark world? (See Matthew 5:44.) If we become angry, we will be rendered not only ineffective but also damaging to other people's view of God. The same is true for hiding, yet I fear we will not see the consequences of our hiding until it is too late. Hiding equates to denying that we know Christ, and if we deny Christ before man, He will deny knowing us before His Father. (See Matthew 10:33.)

If we never strive to know God, and we do not openly reveal His life in our lives here on earth, when we stand before God at His judgment seat, He will say He never knew us. The message in the Bible on this topic is nonnegotiable and its truth unrelenting. Everything we do—every word and action—matters and has eternal significance. He wants us to allow Him to live openly and actively through us.

We are not here to bring the world to God, but to bring God to the world. He is with us, living in us, and He will go with us wherever He sends us. We have no idea whom His Spirit is preparing to answer His call, so we need to be open to go where and to whomever He leads us. This calling is not limited to a few missionaries or ministers—we are *all* called to obey Christ's leading and take Him into every situation (jobs, relationships, random daily tasks, and so on).

In many of the areas addressed in this book, God is still working in me, and He will continue to perfect me until the day of Jesus's coming. I am not perfect, and I understand the struggle and wrestle with it daily. But in the midst of this, I know God is bringing me to a better understanding of who He is. In turn, I better understand how He wants to work in my life for others.

Is It Safe?

Yes … and no.

What Does *Safe* Mean?

Anywhere with the Lord is safe, but maybe not in the way that we expect. God never said that we would live comfortable, safe lives or that we would never experience hunger or pain. Most of Jesus's disciples died for their belief in Christ, but I would consider them as having been safe. They were safe in Christ, which is the only safety that matters.

Jesus says, "For he who wants to save his life will lose it and he who loses his life for Me will save it" (Matthew 16:25). We will all die one day, unless Jesus comes back while we are still alive. In this passage, Jesus is talking about more than our physical death. He is talking about how we should live every day. We should be living our lives like Paul when he said, "Who will separate us from the love of Christ? Will tribulation, or distress, or persecution, or famine, or nakedness, or peril, or sword? Just as it is written, 'For Your sake we are being put to death all day long; we were considered as sheep to be slaughtered.' But in all these things we overwhelmingly conquer through Him who loved us" (Romans 8:36–37).

We might be persecuted, starving, in distress, or many other things that could constitute "being put to death all day long." But these things will never separate us from God's love, so we "overwhelmingly conquer"—and thus we are safe. "Neither death, nor life, nor angels, nor principalities, nor things present, not things to come, nor powers, nor height, nor depth, nor any other created thing, will be able to separate us from the love of God, which is in Christ Jesus our Lord" (Romans 8:38–39).

Long Lives

We need to accept the fact that our purpose is not to live a long life. Are we willing to die for Him whenever He asks, or are we overly prioritizing our physical safety? God might or might not plan long lives for us, but that should not be our goal or focus. Of course, we shouldn't put ourselves in harm's way just to demonstrate our fanatical love for Christ or do things to injure ourselves. Surely not! We are not to "[p]ut the Lord your God to the test" (Matthew 4:7) by asking Him to protect us on a path to which He has not directed us, even though He often mercifully saves us from our foolish choices.

God often calls us to do things for Him that are sacrificial, anything from buying someone a meal all the way to giving our lives. God doesn't guarantee us a long life or even a tomorrow. It's hard to grasp how short and precious our lives truly are, unless we have been faced with death or someone close to us has. We are to make every day of our lives count, whether in our personal walk with the Lord or through serving others. We should not be looking to see what we can gain for ourselves, but what we can gain for Him.

Vulnerability

Loving the people around us will come with its challenges and painful times. Part of this challenge is how vulnerable we have to become. No one likes being hurt, so to preserve ourselves, we want to hide the true and personal parts of who we are. Yet just as Jesus was made bare for the world to see, naked on the cross, we must be willing to bare our true selves to the world so people can be drawn by the love they see in us. People who are truly seeking answers in life are often more sensitive to lies and deception. If they sense any form of deceit, which hiding who we are can be perceived this way, they will not be drawn to Him but be easily repulsed by us. They might find another person or place that will speak the life of Christ to them, but Jesus will not be able to use us to draw them. God will find a way to bring those who are seeking Him to Himself, but if we want to be a part of the process, we must be willing to be real, honest, and loving. We must be willing to be as vulnerable as Christ and let others choose to respond to His calling.

When I was writing the previous paragraph about the importance of being vulnerable and reject-able to others, I was sitting at a sandwich shop and looked up to see an old man eating by himself. All of a sudden I felt God say, "Go talk to him." I was like, "Uh, no. That would be weird." But His reply was, "I thought you were just talking about being vulnerable and reject-able. Now it's time to put it into practice." *Oh my.* At that moment I told the Lord that if He really wanted me to go up and talk to this man, I needed the "feeling" that I should talk with him to get stronger and stronger. Well, it did—until I was about shaking in my seat. So I went up to him and introduced myself, and we talked for a few minutes. We exchanged numbers and have had lunch together multiple times since. I found out that he is a Christian and was lonely and had been asking God for someone to help him out. He wanted a person to talk to. I have enjoyed our times out together. It was sweet to see how, by being vulnerable, I was allowed the privilege of blessing this man's life. I pray that God will continue to use this relationship for His glory.

When doing something like this in our world, we need to do it with caution. It is important to start learning to recognize His voice in our private personal time with Him. As we practice listening to His voice, we will be able to discern what He is telling us to do, and when and where to do it. When He calls, we need to follow through, no matter how it looks. He is with us wherever He sends us. "Do not fear, for I have redeemed you; I have called you by name; you are Mine! When you pass through the waters, I will be with you; and through the rivers, they will not overflow you. When you walk through the fire, you will not be scorched, nor will the flame burn you" (Isaiah 43:1–2).

He not only is with us but will guard all of us, including the vulnerable parts of us. When we become vulnerable with someone, we are giving him or her a level of our trust. When we trust someone completely, we are willing to be completely vulnerable with that person. God should be the one in whom we put all our trust. "In God I have put my trust, I shall not be afraid. What can man do to me?" (Psalm 56:11).

When we have truly become deeply vulnerable with God, we can more easily be vulnerable with other people, because we are safe in who God says we are and we find our value in Him alone, not in the opinions of the people around us.

Christ's Beauty

Show people the beauty of Christ in you. God wants us to emanate His love, and by doing so we will draw others to Him. It will require living in the grace of Christ. Jesus says in John 13:34–35, "A new commandment I give to you, that you love one another, even as I have loved you, that you also love one another. By this all men will know that you are My disciples, if you have love for one another." He is talking about loving each other—our brothers and sisters in Christ, which will draw the world around us to the beauty of this love in Christ. This is a complete, holy, sacrificial, and pure love, not the seductive, sensual love of this world. His love is kind, sincere, passionate, yet gentle. It turns the other cheek and does not get angry when abused, but lays all of its desires at the foot of the cross. This love chooses to serve Christ and therefore to serve others.

9

COMMUNITY

Let us draw near with a sincere heart
in full assurance of faith,
having our hearts sprinkled clean from an evil conscience
and our bodies washed with pure water.
Let us hold fast the confession of our hope
without wavering, for He who promised is faithful;
and let us consider how to stimulate one another
to love and good deeds,
not forsaking our own assembling together,
as is the habit of some,
but encouraging one another;
and all the more as you see the day drawing near.

—Hebrews 10:22–25

What Is Community?

We tend to think of our community as either the place where we live or the group of people with whom we spend our lives. In this section, we're focused on the latter form of community. Until we understand the importance of being part of a close-knit community of people who love Jesus, we will struggle with how to be lovingly involved with non-Christians. We need to personally engage with a group of believers who can help us keep Jesus as our top desire. We need this community to comfort us when we are in need and lovingly correct us when we stray. With a community of fellow Christians, we can learn to take our eyes off ourselves and personal issues, and focus instead on what other people are going through. Our communities also discourage us from becoming stagnant in our walk with Christ—and, by extension, in our lives.

In the New Testament, the community of believers is depicted as fellowshipping together, building each other up, admonishing each other to be better, and helping each other when there was a need. The books of Acts and Romans talk in many places about the things the early church was doing for its community. For example, they would help each other with needs, giving from their excess whatever they had to help others. (See Acts 4:34.) They were encouraged by the apostles to help each other live like the people Jesus died for them to be. Proverbs 27:17 says, "Iron sharpens iron, so one man sharpens another."

I don't want to stay the same, or lose any ground in the things I have learned or the person I am becoming. I want to push forward. As Paul says, "Reaching forward to what lies ahead, I press on toward the goal" (Philippians 3:13–14). In this passage from Philippians, Paul is writing to the community of believers about the importance of learning from each other and encouraging each other to run the race of life, just as he was doing. We are to sharpen each other so we will become our best, the people God created us to be.

Just like anything else worth doing, this process sometimes results in amazing victories. At other times, when we don't make good choices, we need to be reminded that we can come to Jesus, repent, and ask for forgiveness. He is always faithful to right what is wrong in us, when we come to Him. Jesus has purchased our victory in this life and the next. We need only to believe in Him and what He has done for us—and then live like we believe it. Along with a personal relationship with Jesus Christ, our community of Jesus believers strengthens us and encourages us to stay on the path God has set before us.

Is Community Really Important?

How can the finger function without the arm, or the blood without the liver? As the church, we are all part of the same body. (See 1 Corinthians 12:27.) We are to function in unity, and yet that is one thing we do not often do well. If you look at the history of the church, you will see fluctuations in our ability to successfully function in unity. This is because Satan knows we are stronger when we are unified, so he will do *anything* to diminish our unity.

Unity was one of the last things Jesus asked His Father to grant us before He was betrayed. In a beautifully powerful passage, Jesus says, "For those also who believe in Me through their word; that they may all be one; even as You, Father, are in Me and I in You, that they also may be in Us, so that the world may believe that You sent Me" (John 17:20–21). We have been given the example of the triune unity of God as a guide in how we should live with other followers of Christ.

For years, I thought that I didn't need to go to church or invest in the lives of other Christians. I remember one of my brothers telling me, many years ago, "Ruth, everyone needs community. You can't do this alone." Those words haunted me through the years, but I didn't want to recognize their truth. I remember thinking that maybe I was an exception. In my heart I knew he was right, but still I hoped that all I really needed was God. I knew that if I was stuck on an island all alone, I would be able to live fully, because God is the giver and sustainer of life. But rather than leaving me on an island, isolated from other people, God chose to surround me with people who could help me in my walk with Him and to give me opportunities to help them in return. Because of my laziness and fear of being hurt, I avoided this type of group of people for years, thus losing the opportunity for many years of growth and wasting the positive effect my life could have had on other people. Granted I do believe God can and loves to redeem the time and opportunities we have missed if we come to Him. He has done this in my life many times.

We must recognize how important it is to have this community if we really want to grow in Christ. If this doesn't make sense to you right now, or it isn't awakening understanding in you, just ask God what He wants you to hear through this chapter. Ask Him to open your heart to what He desires for the community in your life.

One of the big things with which our community helps us is learning how to be more like Christ by helping other people. It also helps us see God's big plan, by getting our eyes off of ourselves. When we choose things that only we want, that feel good only to us, or that are more convenient for us than for other people—or even when we look at situations from only our perspective—we are revealing our selfish hearts. Even when we consider our own desires before the desires of other people, our eyes are selfishly focused on ourselves. In our culture, it's easy to become isolated in our own little worlds by focusing on ourselves. We need to be reminded that, as the poet John Donne wrote, "No man is an island." This little world of self is a dangerous place of isolation in which we can easily get lost.

People who cut themselves off from community tend to become stagnant and then putrefy. Have you ever seen a pool of water that doesn't have an outlet? I remember seeing flowerpots when I was a kid in Mississippi, where it was hot and super humid. These pots would gather water and then sit for days, not drying up because of the humidity. After a few days you could see little things swimming in the water. The water would get scummy around the edges, the pots would fill with mold, and mosquitos would start to hatch. (I still wonder why God created mosquitos …) As Christians, we are filled with the presence and teachings of the Holy Spirit, like a flowerpot filled with clean water. But if the Holy Spirit has nowhere to move and flow, we will become stagnant, just like those flowerpots from my childhood.

When our lives are isolated, we become self-absorbed and lose sight of God's desire for the world around us. We become stagnant, and our company is no longer inviting or refreshing to other people or even to God. We need to be constantly moving, filled and emptied by the Holy

Spirit. When our lives stagnate, we need to completely empty ourselves at the feet of Jesus. Nothing less will do. God calls us to empty out our sins and choose to live in His righteousness and beauty. He loves when we come to Him, and no matter how stagnant and ugly we might look at that moment, He loves us deeply and He knows whom He created us to be.

Just like flowerpots during a dry season, if we aren't filled again and again with the teachings of Christ—His love, righteousness, and mercy—eventually we dry up and our lives don't encompass the "rivers of living water" (John 7:38) that are supposed to spring up in us.

Why Is Community Such a Challenge?

Unfortunately, communities haven't been overly encouraged in the last few years. People used to know their neighbors and the people worshipping alongside them in church. There used to be much more emphasis on helping your neighbor and being involved in other people's lives. But now we have a tendency to think that we can do everything on our own. We fear that asking others for help is a sign of weakness, or maybe they won't understand why we are going through certain things. For example, friends have told me that when their car broke down, they didn't want to bother any of their friends to help them, so they called a taxi to take them home. It is sad that our expectations for others are so low that we don't ask our friends for help. When I was in college and didn't own a car, I didn't like to ask for rides because I hated the feeling of being an inconvenience to others.

Yet we should be happy to help other people. Life shouldn't be so much about ourselves that we aren't available to help those in need. If someone asks me for a ride, even if it messes up my own plans, I am glad to assist them. But if we're willing to help others, why are we not willing to ask for the same type of help for ourselves?

This lack of involvement in the community around us is not limited only to the people with whom we physically live, but is often seen also in the Christian community. Unfortunately, many Christians do not see the importance of being in a giving and sharing Christian community. We feel a desire to hang out with our friends, but not necessarily with Christian brothers and sisters who could help us grow into the people we are meant to be. We fail to recognize that the people with whom we surround ourselves ultimately influence where we end up in life.

If we want to move closer to the heart of God, we need to wisely choose our closest friends from people who share this desire. But if we are okay living what is seen as a normal Christian life, then we don't need to be too particular about our intimate friends. Normalcy is not the standard for which I strive. I want the *best* life, which means personally experiencing more and more of the heart of God. And this requires me to be particular about the people with whom I choose to share my life.

This doesn't mean that we shouldn't have good friends who are at various stages of belief in God. In fact, we should make ourselves available to love all the people in our lives, regardless of where they are spiritually. But if we spend most of our time with people who do not love Jesus deeply, we are setting ourselves up for trouble. Our hearts could grow colder and colder toward Jesus.

In the Bible, Jesus sets an example of how to build circles of friendship in our lives. His innermost circle of friends included Peter, James, and John, but He also lived and worked with all twelve of the disciples. And then there were thousands of people with whom He interacted on a more infrequent basis. We should all intentionally build a small circle of friends with whom to build our relationships with God, but also love and enjoy the many other people in our lives. I have four friends with whom I share my intimate experiences with God, but I have many other friends who are an encouragement to me to love God more, and I hope I am the same for them.

We have an enemy who is looking for any and every way to prevent us from living in a loving, growing community of believers in Jesus.

Satan is doing everything he can to weaken our Christian community, and this includes trying to isolate us into our own little worlds. He has done this so well that most of us don't even know what a true Christian community is supposed to look like anymore.

One way Satan keeps us isolated is by enticing us to be proud of ourselves, and we have become a very prideful people. Because of our pride, we often do not ask for help when we need it. Pride keeps us from choosing to be vulnerable with people closest to us, so we don't deal with our personal issues. Pride often keeps us from speaking correction and life into people we see blindly struggling. When we say to ourselves, "What would they think? They might get angry," and thus decide not to help someone, we are choosing to protect ourselves instead of courageously loving the other person. Everything we say should be said in love, out of a desire for the other person's best, but too often we remain silent.

Many times we choose to be in a community of believers because they make us feel good, which is a natural way to choose any group of friends. But as soon as we don't like the way the community makes us feel, we either leave or try to change the community. This is a sign that we could be too absorbed with what makes us happy and comfortable. Communities should be supportive, of course, but we too easily give up on people and situations because they are difficult. We want easy lives, and if a group in which we are involved doesn't provide this ease, then we want to change it or get rid of the thing that is upsetting us.

We need to learn to recognize this mind-set, because this is not the way to build true godly character. We must be willing to hold tight to the values of friendship and commit to building each other up in the Lord, whether it is easy or not. God loves faithfulness more than we can understand, so much so that Jesus has the name *Faithful* in the book of Revelation. (See Revelation 19:11.) He values our faithfulness to Him and to others who bear the image of Christ, which is *every* person.

I hope we can begin to understand that community is important. The fact that we don't realize our need for something doesn't mean it isn't there. I pray the Lord will open our eyes to our need for unity among believers.

What Is Community Supposed to Look Like?

> For there was not a needy person among them, for all who were owners of land or houses would sell them and bring the proceeds of the sales and lay them at the apostles' feet, and they would be distributed to each as any had need.
>
> —Acts 4:34–35

We are to give the 10 percent back to God, and He clearly states the importance of doing so. (See Hebrews 7:5, Luke 11:42, Matthew 5:17–19.) But as He leads, we also are to give our excess to those in need. (See 2 Corinthians 8.)

In many ways, it is helpful to inventory our lives. For example, let's look at our possessions. How many of us have so many shoes that we never wear half of them? Or purses and clothes that just sit there and never get used? We live in a culture of excess, but we keep crying out for more. Instead of continuing to accumulate things we don't really need, we should open our eyes to how we could put what we already have to better use. The scriptures tell us over and over that we are stewards, not owners, because everything we have belongs to God. We can use things to make ourselves more comfortable, or we can choose to use them to help others and show God's love to them.

We all have a desire to be comfortable and provide for our futures, but God tells us to look at the lilies of the field or the birds of the air. They have enough. Will He not do even more for you? (See Matthew 6:25–34.) As children of God, we should look for ways to be generous with our money, possessions, and love toward others and not hoard them worrying about our tomorrows. We should not be foolish with our money, but we should also not buy into the mind set of our culture which says everything should be about the all-important *me*. As we draw closer to God, we become more like Jesus, who *is* love. He embodied love so completely that He held nothing back, not even His own life. We don't need to be martyrs or randomly give away everything we have, but we should be willing and ready to identify with Christ in *all* areas, whether they are obviously joyous ones or not.

For the past year, God has been reminding me that the things in my life don't really belong to me. He has asked me to share, give away, and sell many of the things with which He has blessed me. For instance, recently a friend of mine told me that she was worried about how she would get to work over the weekend because her car had just been impounded. Just as I realized that I'd be out of town on the days when she needed a car, out of my mouth came the words, "You can borrow my car." Immediately I thought, *What just happened? Did I say that? Am I really going to let her take my car for a weekend?* Normally I am a control freak with my things, especially those that are more valuable. I don't let other people drive my car, let alone borrow it.

However, I recognized God's hand in this, because He had been intently working with me on giving Him control of my possessions. So I internally committed to what I had already verbally offered to my friend, and it was a joy to bless my friend through something with which God had blessed me. The things in my life are not really mine. My job is just to steward them for God. My life and possessions are meant to be a blessing to me and to others, but most of all to Him.

Some people might think I'm endorsing socialism, but that's not true. I do not believe everyone should be forced into living the same as everyone else or owning the same things. We should be allowed to choose, from our hearts, to serve others with our lives and possessions as God directs. How does He want us to daily use the resources we have? How can we bless Him and others with our possessions?

The scriptures tell us that God loves a cheerful giver. (See 2 Corinthians 9:7.) We are to do everything as unto the Lord, sharing our time and resources with other people in the same spirit of reverence with which we bring them to God. This can be more challenging with some people than others, as I was recently reminded while working with a patient in my capacity as an ER nurse. The patient was being overly needy and critical, tossing around judgments and prideful comments to my colleagues, but all the while telling everyone that she was a Christian. A part of me wanted to tell her that she wasn't being a good representative of Christ, but she was my patient and I needed to serve her with heart and mind. I kept praying for God to give me love for her and to help me treat her like I would Christ.

As her treatment drew to a close, I felt I should pray with her, but I didn't know when or where. Finally, as I was assisting her into her car, she asked me to keep her in my prayers. I offered to pray with her right then and there, and so we did. I was thankful the Lord kept me focused on working from a serving heart, doing all as for Him. Without Christ's help, I would have been very judgmental in thought and eventually in prayer, but He walked me through it all. To this day, when led by the Holy Spirit, I am still hoping and praying He will open her eyes to His truth. He is the only One who can.

How Do We Proceed?

The members of a community should be overflowing with love for God and each other. With love and humility, our community can help us heal and thrive. The process of developing and living in a community of believers has many facets. As in the New Testament, we should come together and share our testimonies about what God is teaching us and doing through us. Getting together for meals is great for building a community, although some communities are better at this than others. Our community of believers should also prod us along in the Lord and help to correct us. Most of us don't like the idea of correction, but the

Bible clearly says that the Lord corrects those He loves. (See Proverbs 3:12, Hebrews 12:6, Revelation 3:12.)

In 2 Timothy 2:24–26, Paul writes, "The Lord's bond-servant must not be quarrelsome, but be kind to all, able to teach, patient when wronged, with gentleness correcting those who are in opposition, if perhaps God may grant them repentance leading to the knowledge of the truth, and they may come to their senses and escape from the snare of the devil, having been held captive by him to do his will." This passage teaches us several important things. First, if we are doing the will of the Father through the indwelling of the Holy Spirit because we freely choose to love and serve the Lord, then we are bond-servants of Christ. Second, we do not always make good choices. Each of us has things in our lives that stand against Jesus being our Lord, things that need to be worked out of us. Third, we are to be open to correction from our brothers and sisters in Christ, and we should be willing to also give such correction when and how the Holy Spirit directs us to do so.

We should do all this in love, remembering we are not any more holy or righteous than anyone else. We have all been redeemed from sin, and we should not forget this when going to a brother or sister in Christ to offer correction. We should deal with the plank in our own eye first, before helping with the speck in someone else's eye. (See Matthew 7:3.) Only then will we really be able to offer correction in love.

I try to look at my own heart and actions before I talk to the other person about theirs. Have I done the same thing at times? Do I know the motive behind what they did? How would I honestly have handled their situation? This not only shows me the condition of my own heart buthelps me stay humble when presenting an issue with a friend.

These days, people are quick to say, "Don't judge me." But this attitude robs us of the vulnerability in which the body of Christ is meant to thrive. We shouldn't judge others in the way the non-believing world does, but we should be aware of areas in which our brothers and sisters in Christ are struggling. We should do as the scripture says: "Brethren, even if a man is caught in any trespass, you who are spiritual, restore such a one in a spirit of gentleness; each one looking to yourself, lest you too be tempted. Bear one another's burdens, and thus fulfill the law of Christ" (Galatians 6:1–2).

The scriptures encourage us to love one another through our struggles with sin. Paul encourages us not only to do this with humility, but also to recognize the sin of a brother and sister in Christ as if we have some ownership in it. We are to bear each other's burdens, reminded that we are in this battle against sin together. I might be weak in one area, while you are weak in another. We need each other.

When we are in a position to offer correction to our sisters and brothers in Christ, we should be sensitive to the Holy Spirit's leading. Most people don't like the idea that others are evaluating what they are doing, but as the body of Christ, we are supposed to be helping each other draw closer to the Lord. Calling out sin in another person's life can be a way of saying, "Hey, I see where you are struggling, and I know it's hard. But there is freedom in Christ if you will choose to give up that sin, repent, and set your eyes on Christ. I will help you in any way I can, but it is your choice to turn from it and be changed."

It is important to know what our heart is really saying to our brother or sister. Are we offering correction in love, or do we just want to point a finger at them? If the latter is true, then we should deal with the log in our own eye first. (See Matthew 7:1–5.) But if we do reach out to our close friends and discuss not only where they are struggling but also where we are struggling, we are refusing to let sin rule in our lives and community. Satan gains power when things are kept hidden, rather than being brought into the light and dealt with. Often the person in sin is not able to see the depths of his or her bondage. We are here to help each other, but this must be done in humility.

As we start to develop our humble community of saints, God will show us how our community can affect the world around us. This can be done in many ways—praying together, serving at a soup kitchen, or just coming up with a way to connect with people in the neighborhood.

Regarding prayer, we can only bring into the community the

strength in prayer we have developed in our own personal, intimate time with the Lord. This doesn't mean that we shouldn't pray in a group of believers until we have developed our own time praying with God, but developing a habit of spending time loving the Lord and getting to know His voice in the stillness of our time alone with Him is paramount. From this relationship with the Lord will grow a love for others, a humility that will help us work patiently with others in the community, and an understanding of how God wants us to put hands and feet to His desire to love others.

Most women love talking and being together with other people, which is great! But when the gathering, eating together, or even sharing stories become more important to us than Jesus, we have gotten lost on a rabbit trail, or we could even be committing idolatry in our hearts. In either case, we need to come back to the true reason for the community. This doesn't mean we shouldn't have times to talk about life and have fun. God created both of those and He wants us to enjoy them. I am only saying that Jesus should always be the subtext of our conversation or time together. Christ is the only way we can be unified in the first place, and unless He remains our focus, our unity will not last. He doesn't have to be the topic of conversation, but He should be present at the heart of it. Maybe He is present in the encouragement you give a friend who is having a relationship problem, or as we listen to a friend talk about an area in which she struggles. When Jesus is our focus, we will want Him in *everything* we do. When Jesus is the focus, everything we do will give Him joy.

Once we have developed our Christian community of believers, together we should start to look for ways to help the world in need around us. Just as a body needs to take care of itself and stay strong, we should devote ourselves first to the body of believers. Then as our body is strengthened, we should engage the world around us through acts of love and offer to help the people who are in need and hurting. We shouldn't wait until our Christian community is strong and thriving before helping the world, but the children of God should be our priority when it comes to supplying needs. From there we should look beyond ourselves and help others as we are directed.

The world around us is hurting and longing for someone to love it. The only difference between us and the world is Jesus. Jesus is love, and He dwells in us through the Holy Spirit. How are we showing Jesus's love to others? Is Jesus's love the focus of our lives? If He is our focus, then how is this focus influencing the world around us? When God calls us to help the people around us, He will make it possible. With Him *all* things are possible, whether we see how He will do this or not. (See Matthew 19:26.)

As a Single Woman

Single women don't have spouses or, usually, kids to consider when making decisions, so we tend to make our lives mostly about ourselves. It's hard not to in our culture, which emphasizes empowering women to be independent and powerful. Sometimes it is hard to remember that as single women, we have unique opportunities to help the world around us that women who are married and/or have children won't have.

Have we blinded ourselves to the needs that surround us every day? Do we not see the opportunities and resources at our fingertips, with which we could be a blessing to others? Are we too focused on what we can buy, who we can hang out with, or even what movie we haven't seen? What is the eternal importance of the things we spend our time and money on? Are we regularly bringing Christ into *all* our circumstances? He should overflow from our lives into the world around us. Whatever is at the heart of who we are, this will be what influences our daily life and choices.

For me, this is not something that came naturally a few years ago. Even though I had been an active Christian for most of my life, I did not start to understand how to serve others or love them as Christ does until He broke through the walls around my heart. God's love for me and my life helped me see how much He desired me to love the people around me. My own selfishness became obvious to me when I saw the disparity between how much God loves other people and how little I love those same people. Every day is an opportunity to show God's love to those around me. Even though I see this more clearly some days than others, I am trying to make it a daily habit, keeping in mind that it is Jesus who loves through me.

One place single women can look for ways to serve is within our churches, which love to have us involved. We are all in different seasons in our lives, and sometimes we need to be resting and healing, rather than serving others. But when possible, we should look for ways to be involved in our home church community. This is important for our personal edification, as well as that of our brothers and sisters in Christ. Everyone gains something when we serve. When Jesus is the foundation for our lives, all other things will flow—loving, serving, giving, and helping.

Let me caution here that if the reason we join a community of believers is to find a guy, then we have the wrong motive at heart. Church is a wonderful place to find a spouse, as many people do. But we can easily get our focus shifted in the wrong direction, especially when a guy is involved. When and if God plans for us to get married, He will provide. But marriage should not be our focus, not even when it comes to getting involved in the church or Christian community. Until Jesus is the only guy for whom we are looking, every other guy will easily become a distraction. As Oswald Chambers says, "No love of the natural heart is safe unless the human heart has been satisfied by God first."[18]

When I have a lonely day, I have learned to go to the Holy Spirit and spend time with God. He eases my loneliness better than I could have ever imagined. I'm still growing and learning to walk with Him more fully every day. Jesus is the only way I have true fulfillment and hope in my life on a daily basis. He is the only one I should be serving

---

[18] Oswald Chambers, *The Quotable Oswald Chambers*, p. 134.

and living for, and it is His love I desire at my core. Nobody else will ever compare to Him or completely satisfy my need to be loved.

Most churches don't really know what to do with single folks, since our lives often contrast sharply with the lives of married people. It can be a challenge to see how we fit in with other people our age who have spouses and kids, and who are immersed in activities geared toward young families. On the other hand, maybe we aren't supposed to fit in. God has placed single people in a very different stage of life from most other people. Perhaps we should be seeking His face and deepening our relationships with Him, so that He can easily guide us to where He wants us to be. God works in ways we don't understand, and there are reasons why we are unmarried. We need to learn what He desires for our lives and how to be faithful stewards of the time He has given us.

How are we supposed to be serving our communities of believers? How is God telling us to use our time, resources, and passions? Our lives have purpose and meaning, and we were put here for such a time as this, just like Esther. (See Esther 4:14.) How are we using the time that God has given to us? Do we know the heartbeat of God and recognize His voice? Will we love Him and follow where and when He leads?

Just as a Reminder

Jesus should be our focus, hope, and passion. From Him, all else will come. He will help us see how to be involved with this community of people who love Jesus. He will show us how to be humble and work with people of differing opinions, if we let Him. This community will never work if we do not come together in the power of Jesus's grace. We all have issues with which we need to deal, rooted in our individual characters and personalities. We are all broken and in need of God's renewal daily.

As Jesus helps us develop humility, which is in a constant battle with our flesh, then He also will help us see our need to be vulnerable with others. When He came to earth, Jesus was completely vulnerable, even though He was God in flesh. He was born as a helpless baby, and then He died on a cross naked for all the world to see. He was showing us how to love others and enjoy true unity with each other, but we must be open and vulnerable. Does this come with risk? Yes, it does, because there is great risk in being vulnerable to other people. But our vulnerability is crucial to the unity of the community of Christ.

If we have found our true worth in Christ, and we have come to the place of being completely vulnerable and poured out to God, then nothing man can do will hurt as deeply ever again. People will continue to say and do things that hurt us. But if we put our complete hope in God and He has become our all, then the hurtful things people throw at us will not penetrate our shield of faith in God. "From my distress I called upon the Lord; The Lord answered me and set me in a large place. The Lord is for me; I will not fear; What can man do to me?" (Psalm 118:5–6).

God is for us! If we truly believe this, it will be evident in our lives. We will truly see who we are in Christ and we will live the lives we are meant to live, believing that "we are more than conquerors through Him who loved us." (Romans 8:37 NKJV) When we believe this—really believe this—we will not fear what people say or do to us. If we believe God's Word, it will change everything. Once again, "If God is for us, who can be against us?" (Romans 8:31 NIV).

10

THE BATTLE IS WON, JUST STAND

Teach me Your way, O Lord,
And lead me in a level path
Because of my foes.
Do not deliver me over to the desires of my adversaries,
For false witnesses have risen against me,
And such as breathe out violence.
I would have despaired unless I had
believed that I would see the goodness of the Lord
In the land of the living.
Wait for the Lord;
Be strong and let your heart take courage;
Yes, wait for the Lord.

—Psalm 27:12–14

Yes, Christ came to earth and died. But then He rose from the dead so that we could have a close relationship with Him, life, forgiveness of sins, righteousness, heaven, freedom, and many other blessings. Our part is to accept Jesus as our Lord and Savior. When we choose Him, He frees us from our sinful natures. Paul says, "For the death that He died, He died to sin once for all; but the life that He lives, He lives to God. Even so consider yourselves to be dead to sin, but alive to God in Christ Jesus" (Romans 6:10–11).

We are no longer slaves to sin, because Christ has given us His nature, over which sin is not master. Jesus has already conquered sin.

Satan has been defeated. Jesus took on Himself the punishment we deserve, and now He gives us the life and freedom that He deserves.

The Deceiver

Satan hates God and, by extension, you and me. Even though he knows he has been defeated, he wants to hurt the heart of God as much as he can. He also knows that one day he will be in hell for eternity, and he doesn't like the idea of suffering alone, so he's trying to take as many people as possible with him. Satan deceives some people by warping their view of God so that they live in rebellion, perhaps without even knowing it. Satan deceives other people by giving them false hope and then making them think it came from God. When these hopes do not come to fruition, they become angry with God and turn away in bitterness.

Satan also confuses people about salvation's true meaning. There is nothing that we can ever do that will add or take away from the sacrifice that Jesus made. "If you confess with your mouth Jesus as Lord, and believe in your heart that God raised Him from the dead, you will be saved" (Romans 10:9). But when we don't actually live like we believe, it creates a problem. True belief exists only when Jesus is given complete authority in our lives and becomes Lord. *Lord* is not a word we use much these days, but it means "one having power and authority over others."[19] When our Lord Jesus says to do something, we are supposed to obey. True salvation means giving God *all* control in our lives, because belief and obedience always work together. (See John 3:36.) Beyond this, there is so much more to walking with Him than just salvation, which is the foundation, not the building. Building our lives with and through Jesus is not drudgery. Indeed, it is a *joy*, because He loves us and always wants to be in closer relationship with us.

Satan also deceives us by telling us that we should be the focus of

---

[19] *Merriam-Webster Dictionary.*

our own lives. It's natural to assume that a life blessed by God will be comfortable and easy, with a nice house and plenty of money in the bank to pay for everything we need and want. In our culture, we don't even think to question our expectations and the thoughts in our heads, which we blindly accept as being *good*. But this is where we can get caught in Satan's trap, because he likes things done in secret and hidden away from notice. This is why he is called *the deceiver*. (See Revelation 12:9.) He doesn't want us to recognize the flaws in our thinking and ask God to help us. Satan wants to destroy our lives any way he can, because he *hates* us. But God *loves* us so much that He "did not spare His own Son, but delivered Him over for us all, [so] how will He not also with Him freely give us all things?" (Romans 8:32).

The Cost

The example to which I keep coming back, which shows the ultimate result of being deceived by Satan, is Jesus's story of the ten virgins with the lamps:

> Then the kingdom of heaven will be comparable to ten virgins, who took their lamps and went out to meet the bridegroom. Five of them were foolish, and five were prudent. For when the foolish took their lamps, they took no oil with them, but the prudent took oil in flasks along with their lamps. Now while the bridegroom was delaying, they all got drowsy and began to sleep. But at midnight there was a shout, "Behold, the bridegroom! Come out to meet *him*." Then all those virgins rose and trimmed their lamps. The foolish said to the prudent, "Give us some of your oil, for our lamps are going out." But the prudent answered, "No, there will not be enough for us and you *too*; go instead to the dealer and buy *some* for yourselves." And while they were going away to make the purchase, the bridegroom came, and those who were ready went in with

him to the wedding feast; and the door was shut. Later the other virgins also came, saying, "Lord, Lord, open up for us." But he answered, "Truly I say to you, I do not know you." Be on the alert then, for you do not know the day nor the hour. (Matthew 25:1–13)

Five of the virgins were foolish, but all ten had lamps, signifying that they all believed in Jesus and His imminent return. And yet the five foolish virgins were willing to give of themselves only what they thought was necessary. They didn't bother to make sure they had enough oil in their lamps until it was too late. The other five virgins, who were more prudent, made sure they had sufficient oil to last until the bridegroom came for them. They didn't wait until they knew the cost before preparing themselves with sufficient oil. They were willing to give whatever it took.

When the bridegroom came, those who were not prepared were not admitted to the banquet, even though they had believed the bridegroom would come. Belief without action is not real belief, because action is the evidence of true belief. We must give our all to be ready for Christ when He returns. (If you want to read another interpretation of this parable, I suggest John Bevere's book *A Heart Ablaze*.)

The Bible includes other stories that speak to our need to give all for God. For example, Jesus told a parable about a man who found a pearl of great price: "Again, the kingdom of heaven is like a merchant seeking fine pearls, and upon finding one pearl of great value, he went and sold all that he had and bought it" (Matthew 13:45–46). Jesus says the kingdom of heaven is like this pearl, and we are that merchant. We can recognize the value of the pearl but not be willing to give all we have to purchase it, or we can be like the merchant in this parable and give everything for the pearl. Jesus has provided the opportunity, but the outcome is up to us. Is He more important, or are we? Let's have the heart to choose Him above everything else, because when we do, all of heaven rejoices. Then we stand in obedient surrender to our King.

What Does It Mean to Stand?

How we stand in our spiritual lives affects the whole of our lives. The degree of our surrender to the Lord is the same degree to which He will be able to work through us. As you've read this book, you've probably noticed that I talk about surrender a lot. Without surrender, you cannot grow in Christ, because He will not be allowed to work fully in your life. And without surrender, you will not experience the true joy of knowing God. There is so much to the journey of life with Him, and it all requires surrender and a dying to our own wills. Sound painful? It can be, but God is worth it. He is worth everything, and He will not require anything from us that He is not willing and able to fill with Himself. Nothing else in our lives can compare to Jesus.

Standing is not a passive thing. In this world, standing in the integrity of Christ and His holiness is a massive challenge. Not only do our selfish desires go against living this way, but we are assaulted on all sides by people or things trying to distract us. Some things dull our senses, so that we don't even know we are becoming complacent or giving in to the culture around us. Standing takes discipline of character and body. In our spirits, we must learn to develop the discipline that will make us strong in the Lord and able to successfully fight our daily battles.

If our bodies have to remain in one position for long, they start to ache. When we stand for a while, our feet begin to hurt and we long to change positions or find a chair in which to sit. From having worked as an ER nurse for years, I know that standing for even twelve hours can be a challenge. Even so, Christ calls us not only to stand, but to stand firm, because there is nothing we are called to do that He has not already done. In Ephesians 6, Paul tells us we need to put on armor and stand against Satan's schemes (Ephesians 6:14). Paul says we are to do everything to stand firm. In fact, he says this twice to emphasize its importance. We are to stand firm, armed and ready for battle, praying constantly in the Spirit. We are to stand firm by daily living in Christ and His attributes, which by their nature fight against the enemy.

Paul says our fight "is not against flesh and blood, but against the rulers, against the powers, against the world forces of this darkness, against the spiritual forces of wickedness in the heavenly places" (Ephesians 6:12). He emphasizes the fact that our fight is not of the natural, but of the spiritual side of life. What is visible now is temporal, but the spirit realm that we can't see is eternal. Our enemy in our daily struggles is not the people around us; it's the evil in spiritual places. We need to be always ready to stand against this enemy.

There is a spiritual aspect to everything we face in our physical lives. In the Old Testament, when Elisha was surrounded by an army of men, his servant was scared. So Elisha prayed that God would open his servant's eyes, and when God did, the servant could see the host of God's spiritual army all around them. (See 2 Kings 6:17.) This army of God was the spiritual aspect of the physical battle being waged. Scriptural examples, like this story of Elisha, help open our eyes to the commingling of the spiritual and physical aspects of our lives.

All things in life, large and small, point us either toward or away from God, whether blatantly or simply by distracting us. What is the point of watching that TV show or listening to that music? Is everything we put before our eyes bringing us closer to the King of kings, or is it numbing us into thinking it is no big deal? Do we even notice the significance of what we are doing? There's nothing inherently wrong with watching television or listening to music. After all, creativity is a gift from God, even though not all creativity is used for His glory. But we need to be aware of how things are influencing us. Even when taking pleasure in something God created, we must be careful.

C. S. Lewis talks about this in *The Screwtape Letters*, a fictional correspondence between an experienced, older demon and his nephew. The older demon is instructing his nephew on how to deceive people:

> Never forget that when we are dealing with any pleasure in
> its healthy and normal and satisfying form, we are, in a sense,

on the Enemy's [God's] ground. I know we have won many a soul through pleasure. All the same, it is His invention, not ours. He [God] made all the pleasures: all our research so far has not enabled us to produce one. All we can do is to encourage the humans to take pleasures which our Enemy has produced, at times, or in ways, or in degrees, which He has forbidden. Hence we always try to work away from the natural condition of any pleasure to that in which it is least natural, least redolent of its Maker, and least pleasurable. An ever increasing craving for an ever diminishing pleasure is the formula."[20] (clarification added)

We must not forget that we have an enemy, Satan, who is fighting against us daily. Satan will do *anything* to prevent us from having a close relationship with our Creator. He will twist anything he can to warp our view of God and who we think we are in Christ. In the scriptures, Satan is said to be a thief who wants only "to steal and kill and destroy" (John 10:10).

A war for people's eternal destinations is waging all around us. If we aren't aware of that, the enemy has blinded us so that our view of what is happening around us spiritually is severely dimmed. Satan doesn't need to fight as hard against a blind soldier, so he will try to keep us that way as long as possible. Awake, oh watchman, arise and shake the dust off, for the victory is the Lord's, but we must stand and be counted.

We strengthen our armor by deepening our relationship with God and knowing who we are in Him. Then our armor will protect us and help us fight effectively in our daily battles and throughout the war. All of the armor mentioned in Ephesians 6 is intended for our protection except for the sword of the Spirit, God's Word, which is our only offensive weapon—along with prayer, which is mentioned later in the same chapter. How can we truly fight well in this war if we do not know the Word of God well enough to use it in our battles? God's Word is living. (See Hebrews 4:12.) We need to learn how to use His

---

[20] C. S. Lewis, *The Screwtape Letters: With, Screwtape Proposes a Toast*, p. 44.

Word the way He wants. We must not allow our culture or lifestyles to weaken our belief in the strength of our armor or the weapons that we use to fight—truth, righteousness, salvation, the word of peace, faith, and the Word of God.

If you are not familiar with the armor mentioned in chapter 6 of Ephesians, I strongly encourage you to read this scripture, pray about it, and spend time working on how it should affect you.

Are we standing firm on God's promises and putting on the armor of God daily? Are we renewing our minds in God's presence and Word daily? Are we standing firm on who He says we are, rather than on who the world says we are? Standing is not a passive thing—it means actively working and moving toward God. When we truly believe what He says about us, we don't want to stay where we are. We want to draw closer to Him, and we want to help this world understand and feel His love. God's love is truly contagious, but how can we share His love with other people until we better grasp the depths of His love for ourselves?

How Do We Stand?

To help us understand how to stand with the Lord, we will now discuss the foundational elements of a walk with God. As we grow in the Lord, we will begin to better understand how important these basic elements really are. A building is only as strong as its foundation, and we need our foundation to remain strong.

Salvation

First and foremost, we must receive the saving work of Jesus on the cross, which means acknowledging our sinfulness, recognizing Jesus as the only way to be forgiven, and acknowledging Him to be our Lord and Savior. In John 14:6, Jesus clearly says, "I am the way, and the truth, and the life; no one comes to the Father but through Me." We must recognize this, choose to accept His gift of forgiveness, and give Him authority in our lives. (See John 3:36, 14:21.) Heaven rejoices over us when we choose Him! (See Luke 15:10.)

Prayer

Prayer is as easy as talking, but how we go about praying can make a huge difference in our lives and the lives of other people. Most inexperienced people worry about what they should say and how they should sound while praying. But in the Sermon on the Mount, when Jesus was asked how we should pray, He gave us the perfect example: "Our Father who is in heaven, Hallowed be Your name. Your kingdom come, Your will be done, on earth as it is in heaven. Give us this day our daily bread. And forgive us our debts, as we have forgiven our debtors. And do not lead us into temptation, but deliver us from evil. [For Yours is the kingdom and the power and the glory forever. Amen]" (Matthew 6:9–13). We can learn so many lessons from this prayer that Jesus offers, including the attitude in which we should come before God, the order in which we should approach His throne, and the things He wants us to talk to Him about.

First, Jesus reminds us about God's desire to be seen as our Father. We are meant to live as children of God, not with a sense of entitlement, but with the confidence that goes hand in hand with being a child of God. Just as some children have close relationships with their fathers, God wants us to have a close relationship with Him. That's why He sent the Holy Spirit to live in us and commune with us.

Second, when Jesus describes God as being "in heaven," He is reminding us that God is high above us (Matthew 6:9). We must remember who God is and that we are nothing compared with Him. We are only what He has chosen to make us, so we should approach Him in reverence, not pride or entitlement. When Jesus tells us to come boldly before God's throne, He doesn't mean for us to do so irreverently.

(See Hebrews 4:16.) Instead, we are to go to God at any time and in any situation, with confidence in God and His love for us.

Next, we should approach God with thanksgiving and worship, as suggested by the words *Hallowed be Your name* (Matthew 6:9). Our priority should not be ourselves, the requests we might have, or the situation we might be in. God wants our hearts to delight in Him, which will be reflected in how we start our time talking with Him. Also, if we use this step of worship only as a highway to get to what we *really* want to talk to Him about, He will know. God is our destination, not the highway by which we get whatever we want. As we grow in the Lord, this will become natural. His praises will overflow with joy like a river.

In Jesus's prayer, He also asks God to bring His kingdom to earth. (See Matthew 6:10.) He wants us to see how the kingdom of heaven is for us here and now, and He wants us to see the importance of asking God to let us and those around us experience the kingdom of God here on earth.

When praying, it is good to ask for God's will to be done, rather than our own. (See Matthew 6:10.) We need to remind ourselves of this daily. We too easily lose sight of His desires and replace them with our own. Praying this way helps us keep our focus on His will.

We should ask for the things we need in life, knowing that God cares about every aspect of our lives. Jesus says that God cares for the birds of the air, and "are you not worth much more than they?" (Matthew 6:26). He will provide our needs, just as He does for other creatures of the earth, but we must "seek first His kingdom and His righteousness, and all these things will be added" (Matthew 6:33).

All our needs will be met, although we must not confuse our needs with our wants. If our hearts are set on God alone, He will take care of the rest.

Then Jesus tells us to ask for forgiveness for our sins, but we must also be careful to forgive others. (See Matthew 6:12.) To the extent that we forgive others, we will be forgiven. If we do not forgive others, however, we will not be forgiven. This is intense but important to take to heart. We are not to harbor any unforgiveness in our hearts. We are to forgive seventy times seven, which really means as often and as many times as necessary, hard as it may be. (See Matthew 18:22.)

The last part of this prayer reminds us to ask God to keep us away from temptation and evil. (See Matthew 6:13.) When we give in to temptation, we are put in bondage by Satan, the evil one, and rendered weak. We will not be able to walk in Jesus's power of redemption if we have been deceived and taken captive by the evil one. Jesus is reminding us to keep our eyes open for temptation and to stay alert for those who will try to deceive us. It is also there to remind us of our need for God's compassion, which is something we need daily and is "new every morning" (Lamentations 3:22–23 NIV).

Finally, the last part of Matthew 6:13 brings it all back to the foundation of worshipping God. He is great, and to Him is "the kingdom and the power and the glory forever. Amen." I have gone through long seasons where I start every day with this prayer while still on my bed. It helps me set my mind on Him for the day from the very beginning.

In Ephesians 6:18, we are taught to "pray at all times in the Spirit." Similarly, Philippians 4:6 tells us to pray about everything: "In everything by pray and supplication with thanksgiving let your requests be made known to God." There are many reasons we should pray, but perhaps the most important reason is that through prayer, we will grow in a relationship with God and learn to hear His voice.

I have a tendency to take things for granted when I do not see their source. Sometimes I take blessings for granted, as if I am somehow entitled to them, and forget to thank God for them. This isn't an intentional oversight; I have simply become accustomed to being blessed. But I have since learned that when I ask God for help or provision, I am constantly reminding myself who is providing for me. Through this I am less likely to forget to thank Him.

Our God is a loving Father who wants to give us good things. The scriptures say, "Every good thing given and every perfect gift is from above, coming down from the Father of lights" (James 1:17). Every good gift that we have is actually from God. Thank you, Lord, for Your kindness toward us!

Scripture

Throughout this book, I have quoted a lot of scripture to support the things I have written. My words are nowhere near as important as the Word of God, because only words inspired by the Holy Spirit have life in them. The Scripture is the inspired work of God, useful for any issue past, present, or future. As Paul says in 2 Timothy 3:16–17, "All Scripture is inspired by God and profitable for teaching, for reproof, for correction, for training in righteousness; so that the man of God may be adequate, equipped for every good work."

Jesus tells us in Matthew 24:35 that God's Word will outlive the heavens and earth. It will never become irrelevant, because it isn't a deceased relic of the past. "The word of God is living and active and sharper than any two-edged sword, and piercing as far as the division of soul and spirit, of both joints and marrow, and able to judge the thoughts and intentions of the heart" (Romans 4:12). God's Word is "a lamp to my feet and a light to my path" (Psalm 119:105).

Even though the scripture is good for all things and powerfully alive, we must act on it and live it out. "Do not merely listen to the word, and so deceive yourselves. Do what it says. Anyone who listens to the word but does not do what it says is like a man who looks at his face in a mirror and, after looking at himself, goes away and immediately forgets what he looks like. But the man who looks intently into the perfect law that gives freedom, and continues to do this, not forgetting what he has heard, but doing it—he will be blessed in what he does" (James 1:22–25 NIV). James doesn't mean that we have to memorize the Bible, which would be impossible for most people. But just as we look in a mirror over and over again to know the details of what our faces look like, we need to go back again and again to the Word of God and remind ourselves of what it says.

Even if we have been reading the scriptures for many years, that does not mean that we no longer need to meditate on God's Word. We need to continue reading and learning from His Word. When we go for a long time without seeing a friend, we forget simple details such as the crinkles in their face and the flecks of color in their eyes. The same thing happens when we do not continually renew our minds in the Word of God. We eventually forget the details, and thus its power in our lives is diminished. We need to be able say, just like the Psalmist, "Your word I have treasured in my heart, that I may not sin against You" (Psalm 119:11).

By spending time in God's Word, we learn what is right and wrong. We gain true knowledge of who God is, who we are, why we are here, what God's desire for us is, what holiness looks like, and how to live in this holiness, among many other things. God's Word is truth, and through truth we are sanctified, which means "to set apart to a sacred purpose or to religious use and to free from sin."[21] (See John 17:17.) We are blessed to have the scriptures available to help us learn and grow, and we should use them well.

Personal Time

We need to train our appetites. Habits are formed by doing things repetitively, and our personal time with the Lord is no different. However, we shouldn't think of this as "creating time" in our day for God, which makes Him sound like an afterthought. We don't "make time" for eating or working, which are far less important activities than spending time with God. But that's exactly how we sometimes treat God—and then we wonder why we don't see Him moving in our lives.

Every Christian wonders what their personal time with the Lord

---

[21] *Merriam-Webster Dictionary.*

is supposed to include. His written Word should be a foundational element of our time with Him, but it's also good to include prayer and personal worship. Reading devotionals or spiritually instructive books, such as the writings of A. W. Tozer or C. S. Lewis, have been helpful for me, as long as they do not replace the Bible.

Many other times God has impressed upon me to be silent in His presence, which can be a challenge. It took a while before I could understand and appreciate this type of encounter, which is a sweet time with the Lord but does not always have immediately seen results. A practice of silence opens our spirits to a secret place of communion with the Spirit of the Lord that most people don't know about. Other people know, but they don't have enough patience and endurance to journey far. While still there are those who have traveled down this road a good distance and can testify to its beauty.

The Spirit of the Lord

My discussion of the Spirit of the Lord is not to be confused with the New Age practice of talking with spirits. I caution you not to try to meld the God of the Bible and His Spirit with a spiritual world outside of biblical context. The Spirit of the Lord is the Spirit that moves and creates life throughout the world, but He is not the trees, clouds, earth, or waters. Nor does the Spirit of God have anything to do with mediums, psychics, séances, horoscopes, palm readers, Ouija boards, or tarot cards. (See 1 Samuel 28.) Any religious or spiritual idea we encounter in life *must* be measured against the Bible. If it does not stand after being tested by the scriptures, then it is not something in which we should be involved.

The Bible says in Deuteronomy 4:2 and Revelation 22:19 that we should not add or take away from Scripture. We can't pick and choose what we want, nor can we add concepts from non-Christian religions to the Word of God. One of Satan's most effective ways of deceiving us is to give us a taste of truth, but then gradually change it until our understanding of God is altered.

Anyone who doesn't want to live in the power of the Holy Spirit is missing out on a huge part of who God is. It is the Holy Spirit that brought life to the world and still imparts this life to every living creature, including you and me. (See Genesis 1:2, Job 33:4.) It is the Spirit of God who gives freedom to our bodies, minds, and spirits, and it is the Holy Spirit who is here now while Jesus is in heaven, sitting at the right hand of God. (See 2 Corinthians 3:17, Mark 16:19.)

Jesus said in the gospel of John that He would send a "Helper," the Holy Spirit. (See John 16:7–10.) Jesus is at the right hand of the Father interceding for us, but it is the Holy Spirit who intervenes on our behalf. (See Romans 8:34.) It is the Holy Spirit who awakens the life of God's Word in our lives and helps us understand it.

Worship

Our lives can be worship to God. Every breath, how we treat others, how we use our time, what we think about, our priorities—every aspect of our lives can bring Him glory. He is worthy of more than we could ever give Him, but it is our honor to give back to Him in surrender and worship. This worship can be in the form of the life we live or the songs we sing Him. We might not be able to sing well, but He doesn't care what our voices sound like. He cares more what's in our hearts than how we sound. If our hearts are full of Him, we will have a hard time holding back His praises. The Psalms show us the heart of David, an avid worshipper and a man after God's own heart. (See Acts 13:22.) Likewise, I want to be as a woman after God's heart, so I sing to Him and show Him my love and thankfulness in how I live and think.

It is through worship that God has shown me lasting freedom from depression, a problem with which I struggled for many years. I first considered killing myself when I was around ten years old. The only reason I didn't go through with it was that I knew how God saw murder and I was afraid that He similarly disapproved of suicide. I put the thought from my mind, but it reappeared randomly for years afterward. I felt mildly depressed most of the time, with no clear sense of purpose or direction in my life. When I graduated from college and moved away from everyone I knew, my depression got worse.

One feeling that was constant throughout those years was the feeling of being uncomfortable in other people's company. I didn't like going out in public without friends or family, my safety net. I was plagued by the fear that other people would think I was ugly or stupid. Even in college I didn't go out and do much of anything, because I always felt criticized by others—whether that was true or not. For many years, a fear of condemnation was ever-present in my thoughts.

Over time, the Lord has broken things off me, including my obsession with feeling condemned and criticized by other people. He showed me—through a reading of the *The Bondage Breaker* by Neil T. Anderson—that these thoughts were not from God and that they needed to be rebuked and silenced. God has been teaching me who I am in Christ and showing me how to stand in His strength. When I was set free, He more intently started to teach me how to worship Him and live a holy life. During this process, He showed me how to deal with the feelings of depression that had settled over me for years.

The Holy Spirit has worked with me on understanding the importance of worshipping God even when I don't feel like it. God is worthy of my praise at any time, no matter how I feel. In challenging situations at work, I would sing a worship song to Him, sometimes even making up my own songs. Sometimes I worship Him in words, telling Him how much I love Him or what I am thankful for. Sometimes I worship God on my knees, and at other times I dance and sing to Him. I started routinely focusing on the idea of God being worthy in any situation that presented itself in my life.

The first morning I put this into practice—while having my quiet time, which I didn't feel like doing because I was depressed—I felt

God's Spirit ask me, "Am I still worthy?" I understood what He was asking me to do. It was time to get up and worship Him, not in a halfhearted or appeasing way, but in a sincere "anything for You, Lord" way. So I got up and started singing to Him, dancing around the room and clapping my hands. (I still wonder if my neighbors heard what was going on.) As I worshipped and praised the Lord, my attitude changed. By the time I finished, my depression had disappeared, which gave me even more motivation to worship Him.

Whether or not worship lifts my depression every time, God is worthy of my praise. As I have learned to live a life of worship and hope in Him, God also has changed my dislike of getting up in the morning, which was probably a by-product of my depression. I used to see no purpose for the day, but now I wake up with joy and hope—joy at the prospect of spending another day with Him, and hope that He will teach me something new and use me to serve others. My days are now filled with joy on a regular basis, instead of being steeped in depression. Praise our God who sets us free!

Fasting

Jesus talks about fasting and says that when He leaves to ascend into heaven, we will have need of fasting. (See Matthew 9:15.) We desperately need Him in our lives, but we do not always feel close to Him. Even though the Holy Spirit is in us and working through us, sometimes we need to make a conscious effort to refocus our hearts and minds on Him. This is where fasting comes in, but it is not the only way fasting is helpful. Sometimes God tells me to fast for a specific person or situation, but more often recently my time of fasting is focused solely on Him. When I mourn for closeness with my Beloved, fasting is one way that gets expressed in my life. The scripture I referred to earlier, in which Jesus talks about fasting, demonstrates this. Jesus says that when He is gone, His disciples will fast, as a type of mourning for Him. Fasting is intended to take us to the end of our fleshly desires and bring us closer to the Lord. When we are weak, He is strong. (See 2 Corinthians 12:9–11.)

I developed a hatred of fasting over the years, partly because I don't like giving up things, including food. But mostly I didn't see any results from fasting, so there didn't seem to be any point in putting myself through it. I didn't realize that I was fasting for the wrong reasons and with the wrong expectations. I fasted only when I wanted an answer from God on a specific matter, which wasn't completely wrong, but I definitely needed to do a few things differently.

First, I did not have a consistently devoted relationship with God. I spent time with Him only when I wanted to, which was not very often. I assumed that was all He required of me in return for answering my prayers. My relationship with God, such as it was, was completely focused on what I could gain. Sometimes I would fast for other reasons, such as weight loss. And even when I did fast, I was lazy about it. I would barely pray, or end up falling asleep as I prayed. Even then, I would get angry because God did not answer my prayers, but I was treating Him like a puppet on a string. Thank You, Lord, for Your grace in bringing me out of this!

I have since learned that fasting is not a cure-all. If our relationship with the Lord is struggling, we need to go to the Lord and give Him whatever we're holding back. Whether it's a negative attitude, a bad habit, an unhealthy relationship, or something else, we need to begin by going to God, repenting, and surrendering all to Him.

Back when I surrendered to the Lord and began turning everything over to Him, I decided to fast about a situation in my life. Actually I was still angry at God because of the many unanswered expectations I had placed on Him, but my sister-in-law strongly encouraged me to fast. My goal in fasting was to get clarity about a relationship in which I was interested, but God answered me in a completely different way, by showing me my unrepentant ways. He also made me aware of how serious it was to Him and how detrimental my unrepentant heart was to myself. He was not going to allow me to view Him as a puppet any longer. I had to choose between myself and God. Now I realize that I needed to stop running from God, before I could possibly think of Him speaking to me about anything else.

Serving

A big part, if not all, of Jesus's ministry here on earth was focused on serving others. He calls us to love Him first, with everything we are and have, and then to love others as ourselves. (See Mark 12:30–31.) Our whole lives should be an act of service to the Lord, whether in our simple daily tasks or in our acts of service to others. "Whatever you do, do your work heartily, as for the Lord rather than for men … It is the Lord Christ whom you serve" (Colossians 3:23–24).

Cultivating a servant's heart for the Lord should be the undercurrent of our lives. We don't always have to go looking for new opportunities to serve others, but we should always have our eyes and hearts open to how we can serve the people around us. Our eyes should be focused on Christ, so that we don't let life get in the way of loving and serving other people. When we are getting a cup of coffee, are our eyes open to the possible needs of those around us? Does someone need something to eat or drink that we could help provide? It is in these basic things that we can constantly bring joy to our Father.

In the upper room, serving was one of the last lessons Jesus taught His disciples before He was crucified. And actually, when you think about His crucifixion, this was the ultimate display of being a servant. "Being found in appearance as a man, He humbled Himself by becoming obedient to the point of death, even death on a cross" (Philippians 2:8).

Not only did the God of the universe come and put on flesh like us, but He chose to be *obedient* to die for us. To serve us in life and death, this was His way. This is the example He has set for us to live by.

Even now He is constantly interceding for us in heaven. (See Hebrews 7:25.) This is a form of service. I know I am daily thankful He is doing this for me. I need His mercy and grace constantly. I also need Him to be there with His blood covering my sins and defending me before the accuser of the brethren (Satan) at God's throne day and night. (See Revelation 12:10.)

The Battle for Your Mind

I am a daydreamer and have been since I was a little child. It was my way to escape to a life I wanted to have. Eventually, this led to inappropriate daydreaming. It was nice to think about the person I liked and feel as though I was loved back. God has since opened my eyes to the verse about looking at a woman with lust and it being the same as committing "adultery with her in his heart" (Matthew 5:28). God said to me, "If you take license in your mind, it is like taking license in real life. That which you lust for in your head shows the matter of your heart, and it is blatant lust nonetheless." One day everything we say, do, and think will be revealed, and this will include the sins of the heart. (See Luke 12:2.) Even Paul says in Romans 2:16, "God will judge the secrets of men through Christ Jesus."

Sister, please be careful in your thought life. We have to keep bringing our minds under His submission. I used to think of this as needing to bring my mind under *my* submission and take authority over it. But I have since learned that I need to surrender to God my mind and all my thoughts. (See 2 Corinthians 10:5.) Every time a thought pops up in my head, I do my best to lay it at His feet and in a sense take my hands off. Sometimes the frequency with which I have to do this can be annoying. But with the commitment to continually surrender all to God, especially this area of our thoughts, there is true freedom in Jesus's name. Eventually the frequency of temptations in this area will decrease, or I will get in the habit of giving God all my thoughts so often that it will be a reflex. It still requires a choice, but the choice with time gets easier. Along with this holy habit is the freedom that comes from covering my thoughts with scriptures on the issue that presents itself. (There are resources for individual topics that other people have compiled. See Beth Moore's book *Praying God's Word*.) We are in a battle for the mind, a serious battle in which our actions reflect our choices in how we fight.

Now if a random inappropriate thought comes, and I know I have not allowed such thoughts for a while, I easily recognize it as an attack from the enemy. Satan will use anything and everything he can to trip us up and make us go back to how we thought before. He may even direct us to something worse by helping us numbly accept a compromise. The mind is not a place where we can allow compromise. It is a hard battleground, and we must not only stand but stand firm. If Satan is tempting you with thoughts that you have not let in for a while and you believed were a thing of the past, it is time for you to rebuke him out loud. Humbly come to Jesus's feet and claim your freedom in Christ. Satan will always try to wheedle his way back in to influencing our thoughts. Maybe we think, *This one time won't be a big deal.* Oh, but Sister, it is a huge deal. It will always be. But even in saying this, there will be times when we let ourselves think more on something than we should. When this happens, it is time for repentance, laying down the way we have chosen and turning to Jesus for forgiveness. We must choose to follow in His ways and thoughts and leave ours behind. Once this is done, "There is now no condemnation for those who are in Christ Jesus" (Romans 8:1).

Sister, keep this one in mind, because if Satan can't make you think in his defiled ways, then he will at least try to make you think of yourself in the worst way possible: by throwing condemning thoughts in your face. Such thoughts are not from God! God will never throw things at you to make you feel bad about yourself, but Satan will. The enemy wants you to have the wrong image of who you are in Christ. If he can trap you with your mind and bind you with his deception, then the rest of your life will suffer. But Christ only ever brings things to mind that will bring you to repentance and into a closer walk with Him. Jesus desires us to be holy just as He is holy. Our thoughts must be submitted to Him for us to fully walk in His holiness.

The Power of the Mind

Satan wants to gain or retain control in your mind and therefore in your heart. Out of the abundance of the heart, the mouth speaks. (See Luke 6:45.) If he can deceive you by planting thoughts or expectations that are not of God in you, then he will take every opportunity to use those deceptions to weaken your view of God and therefore your relationship with the Lord.

In many ways the spiritual battle we are in begins in our minds. Therefore, we must be careful about what we allow ourselves to dwell upon. We should take every thought captive. I am not just talking about the thoughts that we obviously know are not good but *every* thought. (See 2 Corinthians 10:5.) We have to take time to learn about ourselves, which includes learning what we think about. That may sound like a naive thing to say, but I think too many of us do not really know what we think about or what things really influence us. That is because we simply do not take the time to stop and analyze what we put into our minds on a daily basis. We do not stop to think about what we are thinking about. There is a battle being waged for our minds on a daily basis that we don't even recognize most of the time. We need to know for sure which thoughts are ours, which are Satan's, and which are the Holy Spirit's. This is crucial to understanding the battle in our thoughts. If we think that is not a big deal, that is a sign that Satan is already fighting to keep his place in our minds. And Satan does not want to be kept from wreaking havoc in our hearts and minds. He too often deceives his way in, and he will never want to lose any influence he has over us. To kick him out and keep him out, he must be verbally rebuked through the power of Jesus Christ's name as often as is necessary.

Once we understand what things influence our thoughts and desires, we will better be able to understand what has us in bondage and how it got there. After we start to see our need in this area, we can start to give God authority over the things that are holding us in bondage. When we give God authority in areas in which we need for Him to give us freedom, He will do just that: give freedom. Often this freedom requires ripping out an old habit. Most of the time it will not be easy, but He will always help us.

I remember when God asked me whether I would rather watch TV and movies or get to know Him. I was like, "Seriously, I have to choose?" And He basically said, "You are wasting our time with those things that have no worth." Wow! I was so used to watching TV and movies that they had become a big part of how I saw myself. I would spend hours a day, if not days on end, watching things on the Internet or from a rental place. The idea of not watching them anymore made me panic. If I gave them up, I wouldn't know what to do with myself anymore, and maybe who I was would change. I didn't like the idea of the unknown when it came to who I was. Also, in His comment He said I was wasting not only my time, but His too. Not that He is bound to time. But this moment in life He has given me is precious. The time I was meant to spend with Him I was instead wasting on worthless things. I finally chose Him. Not immediately, because it can be hard for me to come to the place of giving up something, especially when it is a strong habit in my life. After making this choice there were times of course when I considered slipping, but every time I did, I went to the Lord and said, "Here I am. Your will be done. Let's be together." This looks different each time, depending on the moving in my spirit. But now I can truly say that He is worth all my time. Also, the clarity and purity of not allowing myself to be constantly inundated by the world around me helps me draw closer to my Love. As a result, He gives me eyes to see the world around me for what it is and how much need it has for my King. The Lord has given me His yoke; it is easy and light. Praise the Lord!

Another thing He has used to help me have clarity and freedom in this is the verse that says, "If your right hand makes you stumble, cut it off and throw it from you; for it is better for you to lose one of the parts of your body, than for your whole body to go to hell" (Matthew 5:30).

We need to deal with the root cause and not only the effects if we want to have a lasting change in our lives. We need to stop putting things in our lives that make it easier for us to sin. Many people (including myself for years) think they can "get away with" watching certain movies, reading certain books, or even hanging out a majority of the time with ungodly friends because they aren't really "that bad" or "they won't change me." They figure that whenever an inappropriate thought comes to their minds or their personal relationship standards start to waver, they need to take those thoughts captive or tighten their laces to rein in the loose decisions that they are making. Yet most people don't think about the fact that their problem didn't start with their thoughts or changing their standards. It all started with what they were putting before their eyes and the influences they were allowing in.

In the last year I have learned that the things I put before my eyes change what I am comfortable with in my own life. These things affect my spiritual life greatly. I had prayed about this and felt the Lord say, "What are you putting before your eyes?" What was I opening doors for? I had been watching TV shows I hadn't thought were bad. But then I started paying attention to the actual content in them. I found bad language, witchcraft, and spiritual stuff outside the healthy context shown in scripture, sexual promiscuity, greed, lust, and entitlement issues, among other things. I was shocked to see how a TV show meant for teens and something I had been desensitized to was full of junk. I was filling my mind and heart with these types of influences, and yet I was expecting it to not really affect me. I was being foolish.

Through this, I wondered why I was struggling with my thought life. Well, why wouldn't it suffer? I was constantly filling my mind with things that were not holy or worthy of a child of God. I noticed that these things directly affected my thought life. I cut them out completely and surrendered this part of myself to God, and within a few weeks, I wasn't having the sexual thoughts and desires I had been having. Also, my sensitivity to the things God calls unholy in the Bible increased. It was easier for me to recognize what things were good for me and what was not.

What Can I Expect?

When you choose God above anything else, you can expect God's working presence in your life. It may not always manifest in the way we typically think—the normal idea of earthly blessings—but He will be there and will be more than you could have imagined.

I remember when God told me, "Never expect to get married." He was trying to work in me an understanding that He needs to be my every fulfillment. He needs to be my every desire. At the time I wasn't at all thrilled with this prospect. It took me some time to surrender my version of an Isaac. Finally, I did. It took small steps of surrender to get ready for this big step. I won't forget what I told God: "Father, I think I am finally to the place of surrendering the desire for a husband, but Lord, You made me as a physical person. I don't see how You can fulfill the need in me to be physically held. Even if I have nothing else, I need the feeling of arms safely surrounding me in a secure hold. Father, maybe You can do this through a form different from what I always expected. Maybe You can send a girlfriend who can be a comfort, or maybe I'll have to wait until I go home to get a hug from my dad. But Father, if You are desiring this surrender from me, provide the arms however You will." At that time, I could never have imagined how God would provide the security that I longed for in a physical way. And I never thought that anything but physical arms would do. But as my walk with the Lord progresses and He shows me the areas in my life that either need to be surrendered to Him and sometimes cut out all together, I have come to experience His presence in ways I would have never imagined. At times He provides such a filling feeling that nothing I have ever experienced in this world could compare with it. His presence is so permeating at times that I have finally found myself saying, "Lord, if I had the choice between arms holding me and being in Your presence, I choose You fully."

What a journey, and it isn't over! Every day if I focus my eyes and heart on the lover of my soul, I can sense Him working in and around me. Some days don't start in ways that are as uplifting as others, but I will choose to praise the King of my heart anyway. As long as He is glorified in the way I live, then everything else in my life will be in its place, under Him. He has the control. He alone can handle it and execute it properly. All to You, my Love!

ACKNOWLEDGMENTS

To the God above and in my heart, thank You for Your love. Thank You for the grace and mercy You chose to give me because You are good. Thank You for giving Your all for a poor soul like mine. Who can fathom the depths of Your love? Thank You for living in and through me every day. Thank You for laying this project on my heart, for the strength to follow through, and for the words to write. May only those words that are from You stand. May You increase!

I also want to thank others for their support through this process. My parents, Karl and Sharon, thank you for living lives that constantly reaffirmed your desire to love and please God. You have been faithful role models, and I pray God may bless you with Himself a hundredfold for how you have honored Him.

Nicole Wilcox, I thank you for constantly encouraging me to seek the Lord and for personally living a humble life before Him. Thank you for praying me through this process, not only with this book but through my life. I will never have words to tell you how much your life has affected mine for God's glory.

Sara Bannerman, I thank God for placing you in my life so that we can walk beside each other. He has woven together our lives, so that we may grow and learn from each other about the grace and passion of God. Thank you for being available for talking, for sharing struggles and joys, and also for undertaking editing and sharing life stories in these pages.

Rachel Clem, my sister here and for eternity, thank you for your gentle heart. I see the love of God shine in your eyes. May it shine for all the world to see. Thank you for editing my horrible grammar and being patient while doing so.

Shelley Clem, thank you for being a constant friend and for being willing to undertake the editing of this project while being a mother of three. I love that God put you in my life.

Jennifer Peacock, thank you, dearie, for being open to talking about life in a real way. You helped open my eyes to the importance of sharing my story and the things God is teaching me.

Naomi Quain, thank you for being patient as I have talked constantly about this project. Thank you for being my Naomi.

Daniel Peterson, thank you for spending time talking about life and this project, and for suggesting reading material that has helped in rounding out my comprehension of God and His love.

Also, thank you to the many speakers and authors who have increased my understanding of who God is and have shown me the first glimpse of living a crucified life for Him. Thank you to all who have been praying me through this. I am eternally grateful. To Him be all the glory!

RESOURCES

Anderson, Neil T. *The Bondage Breaker*. Harvest House Publishers, 2000.

Bevere, John. *A Heart Ablaze: Igniting a Passion for God*. T. Nelson Publishers, 1999.

Bonhoeffer, Dietrich. *The Cost of Discipleship*. Touchstone, 1995.

Bromiley, Geoffrey W. *The International Standard Bible Encyclopedia*. Am. B. Eerdmans Publishing, 1995.

Chambers, Oswald. *The Quotable Oswald Chambers*. Discovery House, 2011.

Chesterton, G. K. *St. Thomas Aquinas*, in *The Collected Works of G. K. Chesterton*. Ed. Rutler Azar and George Marlin. Vol. 2. San Francisco: Ignatius, 1986.

Dictionary.com. "Licentious." http://www.dictionary.com/browse/licentious?s=t.

Donne, John. *Devotions Upon Emergent Occasions. Together with Death's Duel*. Ann Arbor Paperbacks, 1959.

English Oxford Living Dictionaries. "Redeem." https://en.oxforddictionaries.com/definition/redeem.

Gentile, John-Paul, and Jenn Johnson. "In Over My Head." *We Will Not Be Shaken (Live)*, Bethel Music Publishing, 26 Jan. 2015.

Groves, Sara. "You Are the Sun." *Add to the Beauty*, Fair Trade Services, 4 Oct. 2005.

Harvest. "Only one." *Curtains,* Go Forth Sounds, 29 Oct. 2013.

Henry, Matthew. *An Exposition of the Old and New Testaments. Volume I*. Ed. The Rev. George Burder and The Rev. Joseph Hughes, A. M., 1828.

Lewis, C. S. *Letters of C. S. Lewis: Revised and Enlarged Edition*. Harvest, Harcourt, Inc., 1993.

Mere Christianity. San Francisco: HarperSanFrancisco, 2009.

The Screwtape Letters: With, Screwtape Proposes a Toast. New York: HarperOne, 2001.

The Weight of Glory: And Other Addresses. New York: HarperOne, 2001.

Merriam-Webster Dictionary. Merriam-Webster, Incorporated, 2017.

"Grace." https://www.merriam-webster.com/dictionary/grace

"Lord." https://www.merriam-webster.com/dictionary/lord

"Sanctified." https://www.merriam-webster.com/dictionary/sanctified

Moore, Beth. *Praying God's Word.* B&H Publishing Group, 2009.

Pascal, Blaise. *Pensées.* Translated W. F. Trotter, 1660. http://www.leaderu.com/cyber/books/pensees/pensees-SECTION-7.html

Thomas, Gary L. *Sacred Marriage: What If God Designed Marriage to Make Us Holy More Than to Make Us Happy?* Zondervan, 2000.

Tozer, A. W. *The Knowledge of the Holy: The Attributes of God: Their Meaning in the Christian Life.* 31935th edition. HarperOne, 2009.

The Crucified Life: How to Live Out a Deeper Christian Experience. Bethany House Publishers, 2014.

The Pursuit of God. Mockingbird Classics Publishing, 2016.

Wesley, Charles. "Jesus, Lover of My Soul." *The United Methodist Hymnal,* No. 479. United Methodist Publishing House, 1989.

Young & Free. "Energy." *This Is Living EP*, Capitol CMG, Hillsong Music Australia, Sparrow Records, 13 Jan. 2015.

ABOUT THE AUTHOR

Ruth Wilcox, the youngest of four children, was raised in a rural town in South Mississippi. Raised in a Christian home, Ruth was taught the beauty of walking with Christ and dedicated herself to Him from an early age. Living as a single woman, she has worked as an ER nurse across the United States, along with a year in Saudi Arabia. It's in these moments that she has experienced the reality of singleness, both its rewards and difficulties. While walking through these experiences, Ruth has felt God leading her to write this book. Ruth currently resides in Denver, Colorado where she continues her work as an ER nurse and also fulfills a leadership role at her church.

49200307R00115

Made in the USA
San Bernardino, CA
16 May 2017